Dare to be Authentic- Vol. 2

Learning to Love Yourself

Mari Mitchell

DEDICATION

I dedicate this book to those who are looking to be encouraged, inspired, and filled with hope. My intention is that these stories would lift you up and show that there is always a way, sometimes different for each of us and other times so seemingly the same. May you be greatly blessed by this collection of stories written by those who through their struggles learned how to love themselves.

CONTENTS

ACKNOWLEDGMENTS

From the bottom of my heart, I thank each and every author who has contributed to this inspired book. Your courage to participate in this project and willingness to allow yourself to be vulnerable, is to be commended. This book would not exist without your stories.

I thank Penny M. Polokoff-Kreps for her assistance in the editing of this book.

I thank my mentors, healers and encouragers; you know who you are. I thank Universe/The Divine for the spark of inspiration that grew into a fire of love and created the beautiful momentum which propelled this project.

INTRODUCTION

When I received the inspiration for *Dare to be Authentic -Finding Your Authentic Self*, I knew it was to be a series. This second book in the Dare to be Authentic series, *Dare to be Authentic Vol. 2 – Learning to Love Yourself*, was birthed by the great need in this world for self-love. I was inspired to bring together authors to share their true stories of coming to love themselves. The intention of this book is to encourage and bring hope to others, by showing there are many paths to self-love, as well as to happiness, fulfillment, and joy. It is my desire that as you enjoy this book, self-love will either grow stronger in you, or begin to blossom.

Gayle Suzanne

1 THE PATH TO LOVE

Sitting on a rock ledge, watching the ocean waves smash against the cliffs, thinking about authenticity, I am deeply inspired. I'm feeling free and grateful. I am not the same person I used to be. I have transformed into a woman who is confident and self-assured. I have learned to love myself, flaws and all; embracing all the lovely, imperfect nuances that make me special. As I look out and the sun is shining on the twinkling blue water, I feel down deep in my soul that everything is okay just the way it is. I am blessed and thankful.

I did not always feel like this, quite the contrary. I will share an abbreviated journey of my life, which will detail many of my innermost insecurities and dysfunctional behavior. I survived three decades of living a life full of worry, shame, guilt, co-dependency, and fear. In those thirty years, I learned that layers of gunk covered up my authentic self. The demise of a marriage catapulted me into pressing deeply into my core and embracing the process of uncovering the real me.

The beginning of my life was rough. My mother struggled with alcohol abuse, which caused me to suffer from low self-esteem. I was bullied during elementary and middle school, sexually abused at age eleven, and the subject of countless rejections. I desperately wanted to be loved. My love tank was almost empty and I yearned for someone else to fill it up - fill it up so much that it overflowed.

Once eighth grade came to an end, my parents decided that it would be best for me to transfer to an elite private school in the next town. Wisest decision ever. This would be the clean slate I needed. I could transform myself to be anyone. Anyone but me. The ridiculed, shame-based, chubby thirteen year old was blessed with a fresh start. Transitioning to a new high school was the change necessary for me to blossom. I became friends with jocks, brains, druggies, shy kids, and class clowns. I yearned to be the girl every boy wanted to go out with, but was content having actual friends who did not make fun of me. As I reflect back, this was the initial stage of the real Gayle slipping away and being replaced by a Gayle that morphed into whoever anyone wanted. You see, I wanted to have friends so badly that I learned to completely adapt myself to my surroundings. That's what slowly started to happen. I would do and say anything to be liked. I began losing sight of who I was and what I wanted. If they liked blue, I liked blue. If they were hungry, I was hungry. If someone said to jump over a bridge, I'd say how high, after I bought them a sandwich first. If they drove fast, I'd pretend it was cool, even though I held on in terror for dear life.

Fitting in meant lowering my own standards, of course. Smoking and drinking started at thirteen. I remember drinking Southern Comfort right out of the bottle, as each gulp burned the inside of my throat. I did not dare utter a peep as I might become the focus of taunting. Having an addictive personality, my occasional social cigarette turned into a pack a day habit. Several of my friends were intelligent and accomplished, extremely so. In my mind, my role was to be their shadow, always there at a second's notice to uplift and encourage them to a higher ground, although I never expected the same in return. Nor did I receive it.

Gratefully my kind heart and sense of humor remained intact. Compassion was a gift I had received as a result of years of bullying. I might have let my standards slip in certain areas, but refused to engage in malicious gossip or back stabbing. That behavior was not at my core. I sacrificed so much of myself to gain the approval of others, but being mean and nasty to another was a level I was not willing to stoop to. In those situations, I would not conform to please others. Period. I would remain silent. Additionally, I had a knack for telling a funny story and luckily my sense of humor was a quality I never turned my back on. It was the one natural gift I embraced that was effortless and authentic. It drew people to me so I did not need to cover it up with a fake coating. Deep down I knew these two qualities were a big part of me, but they were not enough to convince me to love myself.

I perfected my chameleon persona as I grew older and had friends to hang out with, yet I was miserable on the inside. I intuitively knew in my heart that most of the people in my life were there because I did whatever they wanted, or they sensed I could be easily manipulated. I was obsessed with keeping the peace, even to the point of accepting unacceptable behavior and constantly apologizing for who I was. In other words, I was terrified of confrontation, had absolutely no boundaries, and felt I was to blame for everything, even the weather.

These insecurities and fears kept me from living in my pure essence. These layers of unwanted traits placed a thick film over the real me. The Gayle that God created transformed into a person that was fearful and insecure. When I was around people who were in a bad mood, I automatically felt I did something to anger them. After all, it had to be my fault. What else could it be? I took on stuff I had no business taking on. Having no concept what I was responsible for and what someone else should be accountable for, I took it all. I remained quiet when my instinct nudged me to be convicted in my beliefs. Terrified of being rejected, I agreed with the majority and became completely invisible, not having an independent thought of my own. Being invisible was better than being called out. At the time, I thought it was a smart plan.

When you lose yourself, the essence of who you are whittles away. I do not believe for a second that it was a conscious choice. I believe losing myself was a process that slowly happened over time and it may have occurred because I endured life, instead of enjoying it. Losing me happened because I wanted to be loved. I was open to do what I had to in order to receive love from someone, especially a male.

In my younger years, after I was rejected, it usually led to weeks if not months of sadness and depression. How others behaved and felt about me directly impacted how I felt about myself. What they thought about me became my own truth; without ever taking into consideration that they could be hurting and lashing out, never thinking they were the ones with the issue, not an ounce of thought that the rejection could be in my best interest, and not a shadow of a doubt they could be wrong.

Limiting beliefs are thoughts we have about ourselves that are not necessarily truth. That was what I had been experiencing up to this part of my life. We sometimes believe things that we think are our truth, but are not THE TRUTH.

If someone told me I was a loser, I might have believed it. A statement like that could be seared into my heart and my decisions for the rest of my life. It could certainly hold me back from fulfilling my true life's purpose. Because of the feelings of inadequacy that naturally tag along with a statement like that, I could become paralyzed and never attempt to reach my goals. Why? Because if I believed that I was loser, why bother trying? If I continued with this thinking, the true gifts and talents in me would never be realized, because I believed what someone else said about me. Words can be amazingly powerful and we might convince ourselves that those words are truth for our entire lives. But they are not truth. I had to discover my own beautiful truth

THE PATH TO LOVE

The loneliness and sadness that resulted from my divorce prompted me to make some serious life changes. My motivation to live a healthier life was also triggered by the desire to be a positive role model for my four year old daughter. During therapy sessions I became aware that I had abandoned myself throughout my life. Others rejected me and I followed suit. After this awareness, I made a solid commitment to love myself without blame and without self-destructive thoughts, no matter what. I was open and willing to give myself the love I so deeply craved. How on earth was I going to do that? The following steps were crucial in the journey to uncover my authentic self.

Step 1: Acknowledge my gifts, talents and special qualities. I was not comfortable thinking positively about myself, but I knew this was an absolutely necessary step in my journey. Here is a sample list: I am a good mom, friend, tennis player, provider, hard worker, and animal lover. I am kind, giving, honest, funny, sensitive, compassionate, smart, vulnerable, and easily adaptable.

Writing these qualities out on a note card was beneficial because I carried the list with me to remind myself that I was a good person. My core thoughts were mostly negative, so I had to find a way to stop the negative garbage from filling my mind. Making this list was extremely important. I would pull it out constantly when I was down on myself and it would lift my spirits. I have heard over and over again that God does not make junk. I was not junk. No one is junk. We are all special in our own wonderful way!

Step 2: Discover new activities that will enhance my life. There is a whole big world out there and having one life, just one, I decided that I might as well see what was out there and unearth my passions. I tried the opera, the theater, volunteer work, pottery class, bowling, skiing, skating, book club, traveling, seminars, workshops, African drumming, yoga, belly dancing, racquetball, a new hairstyle, bubble bath, concerts, book signings, swimming, reading, writing, singing, dancing, art gallery, cooking class, massages, acupuncture, game nights, apple picking, hiking, manicure, ball games, little league games, meditation.

I could go on, but I'm certain you get the point. These activities were very beneficial in helping me discover my true passions. Sometimes I would venture out on my own. It was hard at first, but I figured I was going to be with me the rest of my life, so I might as well enjoy my own company. Funny thing is, going at it alone helped me become more confident and self-reliant.

Step 3: Set boundaries. The idea of setting a boundary was so foreign to me. I did not have a clue where to start. At first, the way I learned to set limits was to imitate others. When I was asked to volunteer at a school event and I was pulled in a million directions with other activities, I listened to other mothers decline and repeated the exact same thing. It was unbelievably hard to say 'no' at first but I was running myself ragged putting everyone before me. It had to stop. Politely saying no to the girl scout leader did not make her scream or throw an egg at me, she said "Okay, thanks." and moved on to the next parent. Starting slowly to set reasonable boundaries was a wonderful way for me to test the waters. Eventually I had to set more difficult boundaries and confrontation did occur, but by then I was starting to feel the positive affect of loving myself and became stronger in my convictions. I wasn't as afraid of rejection. Such growth!

Step 4: Detach from negative people. If I was spending a lot of time with someone who complained constantly, was brutally negative, spread malicious gossip and or was mean, I had to take a hard look at that relationship. If they were all about themselves and did not take my feelings into consideration, I had to have the courage to detach from them. Or, in more extreme situations, let them go. Once I began filling my love tank, I realized that some people were not serving my highest good and had no intention of being there for me. I had to spend my time with those that would lift me up and encourage me. That was a choice I had to make. Surrounding myself with loving family and friends was a beautiful gift I gave to myself. My circle became quite a bit smaller, but it was a quality circle and that's the best kind of all.

Step 5: Watch what comes out of my mouth. I made a promise to stop saying negative things about myself and not engage in any gossip. And to take it a step further, verbally stand up for myself or someone else. Paying attention to my words was difficult, but it is on my radar now. I have by no means perfected this step, but I am certainly oodles better than I used to be. Just being aware of how I can instantly dismiss myself or think that "I'm too this" or "I'm not enough that" is so enlightening. I needed to become aware that the negative stuff that spewed out of my mouth did not serve my highest good. I learned to turn those thoughts around into something positive. By making this important shift, I felt so much better about myself!

Step 6: Learn to receive. This is a biggie. Because I felt I was always at the bottom of the barrel, it never dawned on me that someone would want to do something nice for me. But as I changed, the people in my life loved me and were generous. Occasionally they wanted to pick up the tab for lunch. Since in my past I was the one who whipped out my credit card first, I had a very difficult time accepting a gift from someone else. I was so accustomed to being the giver that it never occurred to me to allow others to be the giver. I think of how aggravated I get when someone won't let me do something nice for them and then it reminds me to just let them pay and receive their love.

Step 7: Let it go. Some things are just out of my control. I may crab, whine, complain, manipulate, lie, coerce, beg, and plead to get what I want, but to no avail. It is just not going to happen. I can go around the same scenario a hundred different ways, but it will not change a thing. The situation will not change. The best way to find peace of mind is to accept it. When I try to change something or SOMEONE, I get into trouble because I make myself crazy trying to have it go my way. This is another step that is very hard to grasp, but it works. I believe one of the most loving things I can do for myself is to let that thing go. All things will work out for my good. I need to trust the process of life.

Step 8: Forgive. I always thought forgiving was letting the other person off the hook for the terrible things they did to me. "I'm not forgiving her, she was so mean and nasty." I thought that forgiving meant that I was a doormat, allowing people to walk all over me. For me now, the opposite is true. Forgiving is a favor I do for myself. When I forgive them, I am releasing all the bitterness, resentment, and anger that I have buried inside of me. These emotions when left festering, can cause damage to my physical body and produce negative symptoms. When I forgive, I help myself be at peace. It's a beautiful gift I can freely give to myself.

Step 9: Set aside quiet, alone, time every day. I may meditate for a few minutes, take a walk by myself, or have a good long gut wrenching cry. Being alone helps me connect with my wise inner voice, the little nudging that I get when all is silent and it gently whispers to me. That inner guidance is my truth. Only then am I in touch with the answer that is best for me. I cannot hear my inner voice while grocery shopping or at a park, I need to silence my mind and be still.

Step 10: Commit to loving myself every single day of my life. Whatever I need to do to peel off those layers and get to my authentic self, I commit to doing. Sometimes I'll cry, educate myself, make note cards, tie a ribbon around my finger, anything to remind myself that I am a special, wonderful person and I am committed to loving myself into contentment.

Be blessed and be inspired and most of all, be hopeful!

Gayle Suzanne is a life coach, author of Amazon the Bestseller - *It's in the Little Things,* and a public speaker. She motivates others to learn to live a more content and inspired life. Her messages are packed with humor and hope for others. Please contact her with any questions or comments. She is available for speaking presentations and workshops.

Website: www.gaylesuzanne.com

Email: gayle@gaylesuzanne.com

Cell: 508-981-7368

Susan H. Hutchings

2 LOVING MYSELF
FROM THE INSIDE OUT

My last twenty years has been a tremendous journey of finding my authentic self. Although it wasn't until recently that I switched paths from self-awareness to self-love. My external image was always like a shield for me; my armor so people could not see what was inside. I didn't know how to love myself from within, so I needed to protect my inner self with a polished outer self. I exhausted a lot of energy worrying about how other people viewed me. I spent most of my life working hard on my external image: staying in shape, researching fashion ideas, updating my hairstyle, and maintaining my manicures and pedicures. It took years for me to realize that you cannot control how other people view you. In fact, sometimes putting out that confident energy actually makes people jealous.

I continue to work on my outer self, but I do it for

me now. My passion is being a Pilates instructor and we teach exercises that work from the inside out, like a microwave oven. We work intrinsic muscles to create long, lean lines, instead of superficial bulky muscles. The result is greater flexibility and strength. Loving myself from my center or core has given me the same results. My clarity has improved. I now observe my day and have limited impulse reactions to events that may occur. I can observe my feelings first, then respond appropriately.

I recently started playing tennis and it can be a humbling experience learning a new sport. I was placed on a team a little early for my comfort level. Luckily, my partner and I were starting our tennis careers together. My first impression of playing an actual match was that the game went too fast. I didn't have time to think about my grip, ball placement, and what my legs were supposed to be doing. When I mentioned my challenge to my coach, he simply said, "Slow down the game." At first this didn't make sense to me. But if you relax, (A glass of wine if necessary) clear your mind, and just focus on what the yellow ball is doing, you can actually slow the game down. You become the observer while you are playing. Finally, I understand what it means to "be in the zone."

Loving yourself from the inside is like being in the zone each day. If only I had that knowledge back in high school. I always felt judged and had a fear of making mistakes. I set very high expectations for myself, always being my toughest critic. I excelled in math and science and since I grew up along the space coast of Florida, I wanted to work for the Space Program. I attended Florida Institute of Technology (forty-five miles from the Kennedy Space Center) and pursued aerospace engineering. I remember keeping a journal of my short and long term goals and worked exceptionally hard to start accomplishing them.

As my college career began to unfold, I became painfully aware of my scholarly limitations. I was a straight A student all throughout my academic life, but was not prepared for my engineering classes. It was difficult for me to admit that I could not succeed in engineering, but I chose the next best path which was aviation. I thought I could still achieve my goal of working at the Space Center, learn everything about the aviation world, and maybe even become a pilot.

I excelled in my classes and found a job after graduation at an aviation company near Florida Tech. I learned how to manage an office, inventory aircraft parts, conduct pilot investigations, and promote our aviation services throughout the industry. I loved my job, but my ambitions took over and I wanted more challenges and excitement. I was a long way from the space program I had always wanted and still had a desire to reach beyond my desk job. I asked for more opportunities, but found myself deep in the "good old boys" network. When I hit a few glass ceilings, I remember telling my boss, "I sometimes forget that I'm the girl."

Four years after starting that job, I used the skills I had learned and took a chance. I am naturally a risk taker and was not afraid of my new path at all, excited to start a new adventure. I bought an aviation company called a fixed base operation (FBO) in Laurens, South Carolina. Our services included fueling general aviation aircraft, flight instruction, aircraft maintenance, and a charter operation for passengers and cargo. I earned my private pilot's license and owned my own Cessna 150. I was stretching my wings and wanted to keep growing and learning.

In hindsight I realize that although it seemed like a logical path for me, I was ignoring my true self and pushing even harder to find the success that I had promised myself as a child. I was still suppressing my female energy, focused only on the details of the business and not on nurturing or loving myself. Life began to show its darker side and my linear push to success was starting to bend. I had gotten married right out of college and was terribly unhappy. The perfectionist was doing everything right in my head; not living with someone out of wedlock, buying a house-not renting, working seven days a week to pay the bills, taking care of my husband, dog, and employees before myself. I kept pushing myself harder to keep my image alive of what is successful and perfect. We were unable to conceive a child, adding significantly to the stress I was already under of owning a business and keeping my *happy, all is well,* game face on.

Owning an aviation business introduced me to something I was not expecting, sexual discrimination. The airport commission (six men) rallied against my company creating obstacles for me to grow my business. I wanted to expand the runway, they wanted to keep it small. I wanted to provide jet fuel for larger aircraft, they wanted a self-service pump for their two-seater Cessna's and Pipers. I wanted to grow the airport to create economic opportunities for the community and was very surprised that some residents wanted to close the airport and put cows on the land. After two years of fighting the airport commission, my employees, my husband, and my biological clock, something in me just broke.

I was always in such control of myself and my schedule. I knew every day what I wanted to do, how to spend my money, and what was important to me. I was more serious than most twenty-eight year old women and was driven to achieve my goals and have financial success. I kept up with my daily journal and without even realizing it, had manifested many opportunities and paths for myself. Unfortunately, it didn't include taking care of myself, creating a healthy balance in my life, or nurturing my authentic self. I don't think I even realized that I was a spiritual, human being - not a human "doing". I was so focused on the mission and reaching my goals that I had not even acknowledged a withering spirit that resided in me.

A feminine inner self needed to be nurtured and loved. I was completely unaware of her. How do you discover your inner and authentic self? In my case, it was pretty dramatic. Life came to an abrupt halt. For two months I could not get out of bed, had no idea how to make a decision, and was in a complete state of fear. I resisted any attempts for my doctors to medicate me and had no idea what was happening to my body. Stress manifested in physical pain and I was told it was a classic sign of depression. I told my doctor that I did not have time for depression and labels. "Just tell me how to fix it and I'll go back to work." I was clueless on where to start or how to move forward.

So, my body just stopped functioning. When my physical body stopped functioning, I began praying and journaling my thoughts. Thank God I knew how to pray the rosary because I didn't know how to do anything else at this point. My religion turned into my spirituality and I began to manifest my thoughts in very powerful and tangible ways. I meditated and prayed for $50,000 to get me out of my business and start new. I needed a rebirth if I was ever to be whole again. I tried to sell the business for months and looked for any creative way to recoup my losses, get a divorce, sell my house, and begin a new life.

After a few months, I reached out to a friend that I had met at an aviation conference during my first job. I told him that my business failed, my marriage failed, and I had nowhere to go. I did not want to go home to South Florida as a complete failure. I had created such a picture perfect image of my life and marriage, that I could not face reality, nor my family and friends. My friend Joe literally plucked me out of South Carolina in a King Air turboprop airplane. He lived in Michigan and promised to take care of me while I recovered from whatever was happening with my body, mind, and spirit. I had not given up on my meditation and continued to pray for the sum of money that would help me start fresh again.

Once I was settled in Michigan, I began redefining myself. I started working out, attending mass, and reading every self-help book I could get my hands on. I started talk therapy and it was a huge step in helping me find some footing. I finally started putting myself first and loving myself for the first time ever. It was not until I took these actions that I received a call one day from a school that needed a consultant for Organizational Development and Marketing, for their Aviation Program. They hired me on the spot for a salary of $50,000. Thank you, God! It was the first I discovered that I had the Divine power to manifest miracles in my life. I just needed to be in a place of calm and 100% faith to create that energy.

Joe and I married and I was amazed at how different I felt in my new relationship. In my first marriage I felt like the husband, wife, and mother. Now I felt like the girl. I finally found her! I could spend my day working a little, shopping, and taking care of myself first, not last. I restarted my journaling and meditation, and never again wrote down my goals or ambitions. I just decided to be.

It took me four years to reset my life and discover my authentic self. I was so broken and completely out of touch with my inner being. When I rediscovered my strength, we moved back to South Florida and integrated into my family again. Our families were together and growing with sibling marriages and our nieces and nephews being born. Still unable to conceive, Joe and I had started the paperwork to adopt a baby girl from China. When you are unable to conceive naturally, it takes a lot of decisions and tenacity to create a family. There were many days that I had doubts that we would ever meet our daughter. There is an ancient Chinese Proverb that says, "An invisible red thread connects those destined to meet, regardless of time, place, or circumstances. The thread may stretch or tangle, but never break."

After a year and a half of constant journaling, meditation, and prayer for her health, our bond, and her biological mother, we met our beautiful daughter Elizabeth Rose. It was July 25th, 2005 - Gotcha Day. We spent three weeks in China with an amazing group of adoptive families. Each year, our China group meets on Gotcha Day and we have a huge reunion somewhere in the country. This group has been a source of strength and support for almost ten years. Our daughters are like cousins to each other and they are quite possibly related, although we may never know for sure.

I fell in love with Elizabeth and I love being her mom. While home with her, I pursued my Master's Degree in Business online. I enjoyed going back to school in the technology age. When I had attended Florida Tech in 1990, we did not have personal computers or the internet. I love being a student and this was such a great opportunity for me to learn in a whole new dimension. I did not attach an end result or goal to my MBA degree. I simply wanted to learn something new and sharpen my skills for the new information age. I thought about teaching in the college environment and when a path did not open in that direction, a middle school teaching opportunity presented itself. I began teaching 8th grade Algebra and soon realized that teaching teenagers was way beyond my scope of handling stress. About the same time, Pilates had become popular with the celebrities and fitness community. I started practicing Pilates to counter my stress in the classroom. I had learned my physical and mental boundaries from my days at the FBO and was not willing to go back to that level of anxiety in my life. I fell in love with Pilates. My instructor said my form was very natural since I was a dancer in high school. I also attended yoga classes, but nothing compared to working on the Pilates equipment.

My instructor was starting her own family and asked me to take over her Pilates business. I had left teaching by this time and decided to do what I love, practice and teach others Pilates. I learned about the fitness industry and felt that I had finally found my calling. As a Pilates instructor I was using my teaching, marketing, and nurturing skills. I continued to discover the mind/body connection that is fostered in a Pilates session. Again I did not attach an outcome to my new industry and passion. I just took it one day at a time learning everything I could about the equipment and Pilates community. A local Pilates studio asked me to sub classes and I had a great balance of my small client base and subbing classes. My new schedule allowed me to volunteer at my daughter's school and still take care of myself.

Several years later, I have continued to expand my territories without fear and have my very own Pilates studio. I am a business owner again, but this time around, I am able to observe my surroundings and grow within my own limits. I no longer push myself and recognize when I'm taking on too much of a workload. Teaching Algebra even came back into my life in an online form. I can teach from the comfort of my home, concentrating on the content of the course and my student's success. Education today focuses on the whole child and I am so happy to see that paradigm shift that reaches out to the student's perseverance and grit.

As difficult as the road that led me to this exact moment was, I strive to be a vehicle of faith and hope for those around me. If I did not encounter the struggles that I did in my past, I don't think it would have made me as effective of a teacher and mentor for others. My yoga practice teaches me that I am doing exactly what I should be doing in this moment. My journaling continues to manifest abundance in my life and I would not change anything that has happened in the past. Learning to love myself from the inside out gives me strength, keeps me centered and grateful.

Susan Hutchings is the owner of Pilates Wave in Coral Springs, FL. She is Pilates certified through Balanced Body University and Pilates Method Alliance. She holds a private pilot license, a Bachelor's Degree from Florida Tech in Melbourne, FL, and an MBA from Davenport University. Contact her at www.pilateswavefl.com.

Lorna McCarty

3 LIFE LESSONS LEARNED

"As long as you look for someone else to validate who you are by seeking their approval, you are setting yourself up for disaster. You have to be whole and complete in yourself. No one can give you that. You have to know who you are - what others say is irrelevant." – Nic Sheff

We all have a journey or path we travel. Our life has twists and turns, we make choices some good, some bad. We live through challenges, we rejoice, we cry, we feel disappointment and we find a way to go on. The one thing we do in all these situations - we grow from them. My dad was my biggest fan. He was the first person in my life who taught me to always believe in myself. He told me often that I could do anything I set my mind to. Saying, "I can't," was not an option. I grew up not only believing in possibility, but feeling secure in knowing I could reach out and grab the golden horseshoe. I believed I could have a glorious life as long as I made the effort to get where I was going to and did it with a positive attitude and a loving heart.

I can still remember at the early age of seven, being chosen to participate in a watercolor painting exhibition for child artists at a prominent art gallery in La Jolla, California. All eyes were on me as I stood before an easel, brush in hand, ready to make my best impression. I was a bundle of nerves and excitement, feeling very important that day. It was like being famous for a moment, as I finished my painting and I enjoyed all the ooh's and ah's from friends and family.

As a grade school student I discovered my love of the stage; singing, dancing and speaking. In sixth grade, I sang my heart out as Winnie–the–Pooh, leading Christopher Robin and an entire cast of characters on an expedition around the auditorium. I was fearless and on top of the world when I was on a stage. During my first year in high school, I remember how hard I worked to become student body president. Although I did not win, I believed in the possibility every step of the way. The journey was not only exciting, but it was an amazing learning experience. I again felt myself drawn to the stage and filled with the joy and love of connecting to an audience. That same year, I also went out for the cheerleading squad and shocked the judges during my tryout, as I leaped high into the air and dropped to a full split on the floor. I was bold and unafraid. It was next to impossible for me to sleep that night and it seemed tomorrow would never come. As I was sitting in my advisory period the next morning, I was stunned to hear my name announced as a winner for the cheer squad. My heart raced and I could hardly believe it. A memorable moment in my young life, it raised my self-worth to a new unexpected high.

What does self-love really mean? Some people believe that having self-love means being self-absorbed, unkind to others, and selfish. They may use words such as conceit, egotism, and self-exaltation. However, the true meaning of self-love has nothing to do with how wonderful you may think you are. I believe that a person filled with self-love is more conscious and fully self-driven to take part in the process of helping other people live a more complete and rewarding lifestyle.

From the time I was a very young girl, I naturally fell into being a helper. I had an innate instinct to care for animals and babies, always looking out for them and making sure I was keeping them safe. I loved taking on responsibility and looking after the well-being of others. These actions stayed with me as I grew into adulthood and became a wife and a mother. Many of us appreciate the gifts that surround us, such as the beauty of a sunset. These gifts are easily recognizable if we are only willing to take the time to notice. Hearing a babies' first giggle, the colors of fall leaves on a tree, are some of the gifts that fill me up with love and contentment. It is a true blessing to be able to enjoy and appreciate God's gifts. Our time here is really very short and I have always believed life is truly for the living. We are here to experience what makes us happy. When we can be grateful for who we are, we have achieved self-love.

I remember feeling such self-love one day when I literally bumped into a young lady walking down the street. She was finding her way with a white cane that had a red tip on the end. As she got closer to me and my little brother, who I was giving a ride in his stroller, I realized she was blind. We struck up a conversation that led to, "Why don't you come over to my house for a while?" She eagerly agreed. We soon were inside my home, meeting my mother. It was not normal for me to bring a stranger home, but there was something about this young woman that I felt safe in doing so. When this young lady approached our Story and Clark upright piano, she carefully ran her hand across the top of the keyboard, then slipped onto the bench and began to play. My mother and I looked at each other as though we had just been transported to heaven. I will treasure the gift this incredibly talented human being proceeded to bestow upon us. She easily played through a medley of Chopin, Tchaikovsky, and Bach. Her gift brought tears to both my mother and me. I never saw her again, but the memory of the respect and admiration I felt for her, in that moment, filled my self-love meter to the maximum.

Being your authentic self means loving yourself first. I can't say I've always loved myself. Applying self-love wasn't always the easiest thing to do as I grew up. I was the tallest girl in all of my classes. I towered over all the boys. Square Dancing in sixth grade was embarrassing. My partner's face was at the same level as my chest. By seventh grade I was in braces, my hair was cut too short, and the size of my feet was not in proportion to the rest of my body. They were huge. I remember wishing my hair was long and straight, not short and curly. I wanted little feet and a petite body frame. I was fair skinned and wanted beach brown skin instead. I was never happy with who I was. As I grew older I came to the conclusion that I wasn't the only one who was never satisfied with the way they looked. It took me awhile, but I finally figured out that we are all unique, a much kinder way to look at ourselves. Something many of us fail to see and believe, is that we all have special gifts we alone possess. If you truly believe in the gifts you have, you can help so many people in this world. Not everyone grows up right away or figures out exactly what they want to be for the rest of their lives. Becoming who you want to be is a process. Getting there is the journey we take called life.

My world was rocked when my parents decided it was time to make a major change in our lifestyle at the end of my high school sophomore year. I had gone through all of my schooling so far with the same kids and I was told we were going to start a new life as farmers in a community ninety miles north of Phoenix, Arizona. I wasn't sure how I felt about this move, except that I knew I had to start over in a place that was foreign to me and be the new kid in school. Initially, I was well accepted. Everyone I met in this quiet little valley was warm and caring. I spent a lot of time with a family who lived up the road from us. They invited me frequently to their church and I was so warmly received by this family and the other church members, that I even participated in a musical performance called a "Roadshow."

Unfortunately, the good feelings came to a halt shortly after. I was invited to a back yard pool party and I arrived in shorts and a t-shirt, with my bikini bathing suit worn under my clothes. As I entered the back yard I saw the mothers of my new friends dressed in 1800 period style clothing, complete with bonnets. The girls in the swimming pool did not have swimsuits on, but instead wore tight t-shirts over their bras along with very revealing jean shorts. As I stepped into the pool in my bikini, I felt naked and wanted to cover up. Disapproving eyes were upon me making me feel as if I had done something terribly wrong. But what had I done? At that moment, I didn't like myself much. It was hard to even love myself. The world no longer felt accepting, and living in this place very quickly became a difficult existence for me.

I was fortunate to have a loving family that always stood by me, but despite their support, I no longer felt I could be my authentic self. I was an instant outcast. The warmth and kindness that had been initially showered upon me was a lie. These people wanted me to join their church, but I explained to them I already had my own religion. Because I refused to join them, I was glared at in school and shoved in the hallways between classes. I was shunned and called terrible names. This was the first time I knew what it felt like to be the brunt of prejudice. I was also regularly attacked while riding the bus home from school. Despite my efforts to find a seat on the bus away from these abusive youths, one day I became a human target as they threw rocks at me on the bus. As each rock bounced off the back of my head, I felt ashamed and like an outcast as I tried to hide my tears. Those rocks hurt! I cried out to the bus driver who just said to sit someplace else. I moved my seat, but that didn't help of course. How could the same kids who had been so welcoming initially, now be so against me? It is difficult for me to forget, even today. The hatefulness from these kids destroyed my self-love as I found myself questioning my own self-worth. My father was waiting in his car by the bus stop. He knew instinctually that I had been hurt and after questioning me proceeded to drive after the boys who had thrown the rocks. I felt embarrassed as my dad ran these boys, in their classic Cadillac, off the road. After stopping our farm truck, he leaped out of the driver's seat, pulled the boy behind the wheel out by his shirt collar and put him in his place.

There is a silver lining. I decided to live my life to the fullest, always looking for ways to make life better, concentrate on what was good, rather than what was bad. I was a fighter. Perhaps my father's love for me that day made me a stronger individual. It seemed from that moment on, I never allowed myself to be picked on again. I have always been stubborn and do not give up easily, rarely allowing myself to sink into self-doubt. I pride myself to search for the grain of optimism, to pick myself up again, not be a victim, and to be committed to always do what is right. I am a firm believer in giving people the benefit of the doubt, whether that means giving them a second or third chance. By the way, I did give these bullies an additional chance to redeem themselves, to see reason and admit to me what they were doing was wrong. Unfortunately, they were unwilling.

My first experience with romantic love proved to kick my self-esteem to the curb. My first love often told me, "I love you just the way you are," words from an old Billy Joel song. However, he really didn't love me just as I was. When our relationship finally ended, his parting words stung me to my very core. "I want someone I can walk into a room with, arm in arm, knowing all heads will turn in my direction." Of course I was not that someone. My self-love took a dive that night. I found myself deeply analyzing everything I thought was wrong with me. The loss of my first love was destructive, but I learned with time to regain my own self-love and became a stronger person living through the experience. It was a very long time until I loved again, but somewhere along the path of life I realized how blind and shallow he was. His values were not my values. Losing me was his loss. Moving on without him was my gain.

In order to move forward in life I've always needed goals. Having goals makes me stretch who I am and what I can be for myself and others. I've always wanted to be the best at whatever I pursued. I guess you could say that makes life interesting, sometimes painful, but never dull. In school, I wanted nothing less than an A grade in all academic subjects. An A-minus, was absolutely unacceptable. My mother perceived my drive as a need to be a perfectionist. Despite her perception, I have never seen myself as a perfectionist. I want the best for myself, strive for excellence, have high standards, and give back 150%.

When I was younger, I thought that if I found the answers I needed to have the perfect life, all would be well. But, as we all know, life throws many a curve ball and the answers don't always come when we want them to arrive. We are continually tested. We must be willing to try and try again when we fail and never allow ourselves to get caught up in self-doubt. It can be a tall order to accept this. I have learned it is very human to live life at different speeds. Life is much like a roller coaster. Sometimes we move along chugging slowly, but steady up hill and then we move smoothly along without any twists or turns. There are days where life can be scary and uncertain, or exhilarating and then disappointing. I can't imagine the road of life not having bumpy moments and times of stress. Life is never without its' challenges. Don't stop living your life. Each day is a precious gift. Live, learn, and grow. For when we stop taking in all that life has to offer, our world becomes stagnant and non-productive. I have this continuous desire to improve myself, both mentally and physically. I am a life-long learner and I love to connect and motivate others.

As a licensed educator I found the most important skills I shared with my students was showing them unconditional positive regard. Until recently, I had no idea that this technique is actually credited to a humanist psychologist named Carl Rogers. The basis for this tool is to show unconditional acceptance. In my time with my students I worked with many who had little to no self-love. I always told them that everyone has the ability to shine and each of us shines in our own way. I taught them that self-love requires sometimes taking baby steps. As long as you try to put one foot in front of the other, that is all that truly matters.

Self-love is also related to our sense of purpose and meaning in life. My purpose has always been to inspire others. I have always been self- motivated and I believe in the power of being positive. Life can be gone in an instant. Why waste a moment getting caught up in the negative? It is important to be mindful of self-love. You must feel it not only in your brain, but also in your body and soul. The self-love that is within me provides a sense of value and belonging in the world. I know it is okay to allow myself to feel whatever I want to feel and think whatever I want to think.

Being successful in life requires that you love yourself. The only love that truly matters is the love you feel for yourself and the love God always has for you. Do what you need to do to be you. Find out what makes you feel good and do it as often as you can, living life to the fullest every day. Self-love is accepting who you are flaws and all. It's a lifetime journey, where our experiences continuously move us in the direction of acceptance and change for a more purposeful life.

Lorna McCarty is founder of Phoenix Rising Relationship Coaching in Reno, Nevada. She is an author, speaker, and Certified Professional Coach, who is passionate about what she does for couples and their relationships. She is an ELI-MP (Energy Leadership Index Master Practitioner), earned a Masters' in Education, and has spent a lifetime studying the psychology of human behavior. Lorna is a former Television News anchor and Medical Reporter. She lives with her husband of 26 years and her two beautiful children.

For a complimentary "Rekindle the Passion," Discovery Session go to: www.phoenixrisingrelationships.com
Email: lorna@lornamccarty.com

Lisa Rimas

4 FEARLESSLY LOVING MYSELF

The majority of people struggle with learning how to love themselves. If you can relate, you might be in the same place I was years ago, not knowing where to begin, much less how to love myself. Loving yourself might even feel like a selfish thing to do. You may even experience some guilt around it. Trust me. It's none of those things.

Whether you are a stay at home parent, single, an entrepreneur, or a businessperson, you've likely got "people-pleaser" syndrome. People-pleasing is a very common trait, which we have learned from our childhood and society and is largely responsible for the chronic stress, fatigue, and burnout we feel. Who is really running this show anyway? Perhaps you think you do love yourself, yet in reality, you are further than you can imagine from loving yourself. When we are not loving ourselves and not setting clear boundaries around what we want and don't want, we are susceptible to tons of stress. Toxic stress. We're literally handing over all our power to others, ultimately giving up on ourselves. Falling victim to our circumstances, we feel helpless and powerless. This is natural, especially if you were raised with no boundaries, experienced a rough childhood, or were taught to behave and do what you're told - or else.

I had a turbulent childhood that spiraled into my teens and adulthood. I was the best victim on the planet. Yet, I went from being a "Master Shit Creator" to taking a bold leap of faith and courageously creating a Beautiful Authentic Life of Purpose, Passion, and Divine Connection. When I learned how to love myself, my life transformed in deeply, profound, meaningful ways and became a magical and adventurous journey. I went from depression to divine connection.

My intention writing this chapter is to be vulnerable, raw, and very transparent. I hope that this short story of my life experiences will create awareness, hope, and help you see how foundational and critical self-love is. Let's dive in.

Although I don't remember much of my childhood, I remember just enough to paint the picture of how I made my life a living hell by **not** loving myself, taking care of myself, respecting myself, trusting myself, setting boundaries, and by giving into fear. It caused me years of: unhappiness, unworthiness, emptiness, insecurities, un-fulfillment, not feeling understood, anxiety, depression, self-doubt, guilt, and making really poor choices that led to serious self-sabotage. I was often in trouble with the law. I committed to unloving, unavailable men; some were even married. I escaped by using alcohol, marijuana, sex, shopping sprees, and vacations. I looked to everything outside of myself for validation, instant gratification, and pleasure.

My parents got divorced when I was two and I felt helpless, along with feelings of chaos and confusion. I observed my mother being very emotional, stressed, and quite irrational at times. Now as an adult, I can relate, yet as a young girl I didn't. I clearly remember being around eight and feeling this natural instinct to take care of my mom and make her pain go away. That was a lot for a little girl to take on. I began playing out an adult role, thinking I was responsible for everyone else. I admit, I had my years of escaping and being selfish. I was young, fearless, and living on the edge, unknowingly exploring every which way to sabotage my own happiness. I was on autopilot.

After the divorce, my biological father Mike, who I refer to by first name, had weekend visitation rights. We visited my grandma often and many times he just left me there, going out with his girlfriends and making sure he was back in time to bring me home. He'd ride off on his motorcycle enjoying freedom and having fun. Being a father was not priority for him and even as I write this, a wave of sadness flows through.

The 'perceived' validation of not feeling important to him was experienced throughout most of my adulthood. For me, healing is like peeling back the layer of an onion. Each time something comes up, it's another layer shedding off, allowing me to step that much closer to the truth of who I am at my divine core. Let's back up to my wave of sadness for a moment, so you may witness in real time how incredibly undeniable the power of our thoughts are and how they literally create our experience in every given moment. As I think about *being left at grandmas*, I felt sadness. Sadness so strong that tears are welling up and I feel tension in my shoulders and neck. When I finish this paragraph I'll take a step back to feel the feelings, acknowledge them for what they are, release them, and reconnect with the highest version of myself and who I am at my core, which is Divine Love. I will feel an incredible shift in minutes and come back full of vitality and vibrancy with no tension in my body. I actually just felt a small shift just in writing those words. I promised you transparency!

In knowing as an adult and as a professional coach, that our feelings are only a reflection of our own thinking and NOT our circumstances, I pause and ask myself, "What meaning did I give my thoughts around this experience?" Well, when I was a little girl, I made it mean that I was not important to my biological father. I was not loveable. I was not worthy. I was not good enough for him.

This is where we surrender to believing that all our thoughts are real, not knowing any other way. We get lost and life becomes really hard. At least mine did. My soul was dropped off at the *Lost and Found* at a very young age and it was over thirty years before I found it again. Thankfully I learned later, that in reality, those thoughts I felt were not the truth at all. I made them up and managed to carry all those thoughts and feelings with me throughout most of my adult life. I spiraled downward in a turbulent, wild journey, completely lost and with an invisible backpack over my shoulder. T & F was embroidered on the backpack, "Thoughts & Feelings." Wherever I went, I carried them with me; *I'm Not Good Enough, I'm Not Lovable, I'm Not Worthy.* There was an attachment to these thoughts and they became part of my identity. As life became harder and harder, I became a master at self-sabotage. For decades, I was an expert at everything and anything that kept me further away from the truth of who I really was; eventually compromising my health and taking me to the verge of a nervous breakdown. So now you have a pretty good idea of what I can create with one incident; *being left at grandmas.* Imagine all the shit I was able to create out of hundreds of incidences that were equally hurtful.

And I have barely touched the surface. By the end you will see, and I hope you will laugh and celebrate with me, just how good I was at being a "Master Shit Creator." I say laugh and celebrate because without the ability to master creating shit, the possibility of learning how to fall fiercely and madly in love with myself and experiencing an Authentic Life of Purpose, Passion, and Divine Connection, would have never shown up in the capacity in which I'm about to unveil.

I'm also blessed with positive memories from my childhood. My mother met a wonderful man who became my role model and who I consider my dad to this day. My biological father's visitation rights were taken away from him when I was nine years old. He was free and clear of all back child support, which was part of the agreement to allow my dad, Jerry, to adopt me.

Nine years later, I'm at work and Mike shows up hoping to re-establish a father-daughter relationship. He waited until my shift was over and we talked in his corvette, during which he handed me an envelope containing $1000.00. Unknown to me, this was the beginning of some very hard life lessons that I would be grateful for later. I began working at Mike's company shortly thereafter. I'm very thankful for the business experience. I went from filing papers to being an International Sales Executive. Despite the envy from the other employees, I experienced a luxury lifestyle; a healthy salary, huge bonuses, $10K Christmases, a beautiful home, 5 star restaurants, new cars, fine jewelry, and more vacations in a year than some have in their lifetime.

Somewhere along the way, feelings of emptiness and unhappiness began to surface. Something was missing. How could I feel empty and unhappy with all those "things" right? When I stepped back from all the "stuff" I recognized I was missing love. He did love me in his own way, yet it wasn't a healthy father-daughter relationship. Mike was not capable of loving me. He was only capable of controlling me, and I allowed it. After many years of manipulation and emotional, verbal, and mental abuse, I had a wakeup call and decided I was done letting him control me. I turned down the Rolex watch. I turned down the $65K Lexus convertible. It was all too much of a price to pay. Then one day at work, I learned he was changing my compensation plan outside of our agreement. I had never spoken my mind or stood up for myself with him, allowing him to have all the power. This time, I didn't care anymore. I said, "I cannot believe you would screw your own daughter over money." Three weeks passed and he didn't talk to me. One day the sales manager sat down with me and said, "I cannot believe I am being asked to do this, but your father doesn't see a future for you here and you're fired." *Grandma's house on the weekends* spilled over into over a decade of feeling empty, worthless, undeserving, not lovable and not good enough.

The men I dated validated the same thoughts and feelings. My first love ended up not being the person I thought he was, after over a decade of knowing him. I definitely had some trust issues and by now had built a suit of armor for protection. *You will not hurt me* was added to my invisible backpack.

When my mom and dad retired to Florida in 2004, I felt even more responsibility for taking care of my brother and sister. For over fifteen years, my two siblings suffered from drug addictions, depression, anxiety, suicide attempts, and faced more near death experiences than I would like to remember. When my parents decided to retire to Florida, my brother was just getting out of a detox program. We were very close and I decided to let him move in with me until he got established. One day while cleaning the beds and linens, I uncovered bottles of pain pills hidden under his covers. He had relapsed. I felt scared, sad, and devastated. This was the beginning of four of the most challenging yet life altering years of my life. My brother's drug abuse got worse. The manipulation, the lies, the stealing were devastating. His depression was so severe, that when I came home from work I didn't know whether I would find him dead or alive. Yet, he didn't want help and I couldn't find the strength to kick him out, like everyone told me to do.

So I continued to take care of him. I felt abandoned as a child by Mike, and thought that if I kicked my brother out, I would be abandoning him. I didn't want him to experience the same pain I did, so I took on more pain. I handed over my happiness to my brother. I chose to put his life and his health before my own. Furthermore, I hid most of this from my mother, because she had her own health issues and again I wanted to protect her. Back then, I wasn't even very religious, yet I remember going to bed every night praying with a rosary and then wearing it to bed, begging for His strength.

Fast forward about four years and I was on prescription medication for anxiety and depression and on the verge of a nervous breakdown. I took an eight week leave of absence from work. And yes, I did end up asking my brother to leave, with the support of intense counseling.

My mother was diagnosed with cancer in 2010 and now she had that to deal with on top of her MS. With my mom so ill, I felt the need to protect her and make sure that I was there for my brother and sister if they had a relapse, which they did. My mother did survive the cancer and as of 2014 is a survivor.

Through all the years of struggle and dysfunction I always knew deep down that I had a deeper calling and special gifts to share. I knew I could be a catalyst for greatness. I was not sure at what level, but I had dreams of making a huge difference. I had felt those heart strings being pulled for many years, but fear of the unknown held me back.

At twenty-nine, I engulfed myself in personal development programs with the best of the best and in 2009 I graduated from iPEC as a coach. April of 2013 was my most pivotal turning point. I spent five days sharing the space and beautiful energy of 3000 fellow coaches at a Suzanne Evans event. I said to myself, "This is how I want to feel from now on. This is ME!" It felt surreal simply being an authentic expression of myself. The day before my return home, I had a feeling of dread as I thought about going back to my chaotic life. I had a "knowingness" that I was done with the struggle and it was time for change. My intuition kicked through every fear I had. I didn't know the "HOW." All I knew was, I had to change everything that wasn't working in my life. And that was literally, EVERYTHING.

With loving family support, I took a very bold leap of faith and resigned from a six figure, twenty-five year, corporate career. In forty-five days, I was

Florida bound with Lacie, my five lb. Maltese, and drove 1200 miles south to re-invent my life from the inside-out. I set an intention to open up 100% to self-love, the most profound commitment I have ever made. For years, I was immersed in murky places of my own mental and emotional wounds. This took me on a very intense journey through the layers that I'd created to keep me separated from self-love. With the support of my own loving and amazing professional coach, Angela Moore, who guided me on this intense journey with a loving unconditional heart, I started the process of deep self-inquiry which led to spiritual transformation. I learned that all the love, happiness, and "enoughness" come from within, to no longer looked externally for answers, and how to trust my inner guidance.

I learned how to love and honor myself first. I learned how to be gentle and kind to myself. I learned that money did not buy happiness and how to love toxic people from a distance without feeling guilty. Coupled with intense subconscious reprogramming, I began to let go of every thought and behavior that was not serving me and created new ones that inspired me, fed my soul, and led me to my divine truth, which IS Love. I was introduced to meditation, and also to the law of attraction, as well as to energy work. Understanding how powerful my thoughts were, allowed me to create my life literally by design. No longer was I a victim of my circumstances. I owned up to what I had created and got very clear and intentional around the life I wanted to create. In making different choices, I learned to set healthy boundaries, trust myself again and trust the right people. I learned when to let go of the others and when to walk away. I learned about forgiveness. I learned to give myself permission to be perfectly imperfect. I began to release the need to control people and situations, and in doing so uncovered a very free flowing spirit in me that I fell madly in love with. I learned how to turn my scars into strengths and leverage them to my advantage. I recognize the blessings behind each and every one of them. I feel free in my awakening to all that's possible and I give gratitude.

I'm blessed to have an amazing tribe of spiritually led women to share sacred space with. Sharing one another's unique journeys allowed me to see the beautiful qualities within me on a deeper level and gave me permission to be ME. They have born witness as I embraced a more loving and meaningful relationship with myself, the most loving gift of all. I am grateful to have "arrived" at what I call my *Sweet Spot.* I continue to make my mess my message, help other spiritually led women on their journeys, and continue to grow, expand, and evolve, every moment of every blissful day.

It is my belief that EVERYONE (that means YOU) has all the love they are seeking within. I am fully committed to reminding you of this truth, because I know 100% from personal experience how life-changing it is when you allow this to be your reality. It's normal to have behavioral patterns and 'blocks' that are no longer serving you and when they reveal themselves, these so called 'issues' are just a call for more love. You are worthy.

You have permission to fall fiercely and madly in love with yourself so YOU can learn how to FLY! ~ Fearlessly Love Yourself.

Lisa Rimas is a Transformational Lifestyle Coach and Certified Access Bars Practitioner. Her mission is to help people tap into the true essence of who they are to experience the utter bliss of living an authentic life. Lisa devotes her work to helping woman and men cut through the 'B.S.' that's holding them back. She believes when a person connects their truth and the love that they already are, they transform their life and the world around them. To learn more about Lisa, visit her website at www.LisaRimas.com

Rocky Krogfoss

5 REPROGRAMMING
MY HEART FOR LOVE

It is hard to explain in words what it feels like to experience an emotional breakdown with extreme paranoia and anxiety. I went through it more than twenty years ago and I am the poster boy for what is possible when healing takes place at the core belief level. When you come from a strong male warrior background and you have been taught to operate from fear and logic, you build the mighty walls of Jericho around you. I do not think it would be unfair to say that most men have this wall around their heart and it is the main reason why men can be classified as emotionally unavailable through no fault of their own. As a man experiencing the intense feelings associated with the depths of unworthiness, shame, guilt, anger, resentment, and low self-esteem programming, I felt so incredibly lost and hopeless. These were but a few of the beliefs that reared their ugly head during those dark times.

In my absolute despair, I pretended that I was "Normal", because to talk about these feelings back then, was not a possibility at that time. Ironically, I had manifested a new relationship at the same time and it continued for two years. I struggled mightily to share with my beloved just how I was really feeling. However, I did not have the courage or the faith in that relationship to share my shame, pain, and my feelings. My ego was in constant fear that she would leave me.

I began my healing journey by accident. I was sitting on my bed one night, a full year into the trauma that never seemed to end. Having gone to doctors for help and naturally receiving no healing from those grossly inadequate processes and pills, did help reinforce my understanding that traditional medicine does not know how to deal with such traumas effectively. I will state clearly now, there is no fault in that because these people did the best they could with the limitations of their training and knowledge of emotional imbalances. This includes traditional mindset therapies which in my opinion are ineffective.

As I sat on the end of my bed that fateful night, I accidently but subconsciously said, "Oh my God, I need help!" As I traversed my personal darkness over the many years to come on my spiritual awakening, there was a time when I had a good laugh at the recollection of that moment, because I realized I had put out an AUTHENTIC heartfelt prayer to God and the help I cried out for arrived. This would have been considered heresy when one realizes just how violent and blinding my childhood indoctrination was at the behest of my father's fist. "YOU DIE AND YOU'RE DUST, THAT'S IT! There is no god or angels, that is all bulls**t." That was my teaching.

As is appropriate when you intentionally or in my case unintentionally surrender your pain to the universe, help does arrive. I was infinitely blessed to work with a channeling healer who devoted herself to me in ways that can only be described as karmic love of the highest order. Her phenomenal talents channeling angelic beings, (her Spirit Guide team named Masian Dia) also devoted to my wellbeing, is a gift that I can never repay.

I thus began a journey into the darkest realms of my own inner illusions of my unworthiness. Hundreds of hours of peeling away many, many levels of unworthiness programming generated a journey of freedom that has no description, other than to say: thank you so much to the angels, God, and our wondrous spirit guide angels. Thank you for teaching me about the love I am worthy of. Thank you for teaching me about Authenticity, Forgiveness, Healing, Energy, Empowerment and the Human Journey. Thank you for loving me in absolute non-judgment. Thank you for freeing me from the bondage of the lies my father taught me.

Now you might think I hate my father for what he did or that he deserves the condemnation of behaving in such an inappropriate manner towards his sons. (I was the oldest of five boys) However, the opposite is true today, thanks to higher wisdom about karmic purpose in the unfolding of my purpose in this life. My father did what he agreed to do karmically, for his soul growth and mine. I made peace with his spirit a few years ago, approximately eight years after he crossed over, in a healing that can only be described as miraculous. He has now with my permission, joined me as a member of my spirit team, to observe and learn from my journey for the rest of my time on this planet, in this life. We are at peace and that has generated healings for my wellbeing that are very good for my cellular body and my peace of mind.

If you are holding on to any anger with a family member or anyone, it will serve you well to release it, because these kinds of intense negative feelings are the cause of many life ending diseases. Consider freeing yourself from that life constricting energy and taking a journey into authenticity and freedom.

POWER OF WORDS-REDEFINING AUTHENTICITY

In my experiences as a Healer and Life Coach, there is one characteristic that was mandatory to generate effective healing work. That characteristic is Authenticity. One thing all my clients faced when confronted with being authentic is the overwhelming feeling of resistance. Being human, naturally there is a part of you that resists feeling unworthiness. I have a saying I quote frequently that reflects the reality of heart based healing: "In order to heal it, you must feel it. Run from the feeling, experience no healing." Your Ego has a job to do; keep you safe and resist anything that generates pain. The ego does not want to feel anything because it is not capable of feeling. Opening your heart to feel the feelings is only possible when you are authentic. It takes courage and compassion to feel the feelings because that is the only way to heal unworthiness programming in your cellular body.

Since being authentic was a critical part of my own personal healing process, I became aware of how much we hide, run, cope, deny, and survive in ego mode. I have said many times that I have walked the walk, now I am talking the talk based on real life experiences. When a client comes to me in pain, physical or emotional, I can relate. I will never forget the day I stood over a black vortex and felt the winds of hell blow through my body. When you have been that close to leaving, you are compassionate with everyone's pain.

I came across an article on LinkedIn and it drew me into higher wisdom mode. I can be so geeky when it comes to this, but it turns my crank, so to speak. The words that appeared on a beautiful saying came from Mahatma Gandhi, a personal hero of mine. It read, "I never met a strong person with an easy past." While this appeared to describe me, I had an epiphany: "I am not strong. I just spent twenty years letting go of being STRONG, what I like now is being POWERFUL." What's the difference? My training in the power of words and the frequency they generate kicked in and I chose to send a reworded version of it. This is what I said, "I never met a powerful person who did not understand that being strong is an outdated mindset. Being authentic about your past, with love and forgiveness, takes infinitely more courage than being strong."

From my perspective and in my experiences, "Authenticity is the ability to see ones unworthiness programming WITHOUT judgment of self or others. It is the ability to be 100% honest in the discovery process of feeling the feelings, no matter how uncomfortable they are." Authenticity has been given all kinds of negative labels in our society from those who are unaware of its power. Shifting your mindset to view authenticity as a gift will help you experience it as a gateway to freedom on your healing journey, rather than a trip to the tar sands. Just like a computer, your cellular body and DNA have been programmed with information you learned from your parents, and society. This information contains one of two major categories - worthiness or unworthiness. All other emotions fall under these categories.

When I talk about being authentic what I am really saying is, it is okay to allow your intuition to tap into your awareness of how much guilt, anger, shame, resentment, and other negative emotions you are carrying in your programming. The healing secret is to be free of self- judgment in that process. We have a tendency to blame ourselves, or project our pain outside of ourselves, in order to hide from those uncomfortable feelings about our life experiences. Practically speaking, all that does is add another layer of negativity to the pile that already exists. Coping, hiding, medicating, and surviving are not healing. Without Authenticity and the awareness it creates, you will remain stuck in an illusionary state of experiencing physical or mental pain that you DON'T want. Do you want to continue on the cycle of pain? Of course not, but that is what you are doing.

Let's talk about The Law of Attraction now. Authenticity and the Law of Attraction- what has one got to do with the other? The Law of Attraction simply states that whatever you BELIEVE about yourself transmits a magnetic energy signal out into the world that will always come back to you in mirrored life experiences. So, if you are angry, you can expect to attract more reasons to be angry. If you know this, then why not choose to release the root cause of the cycle of anger experiences by being authentic about the REAL source of your anger; your past programming of unworthiness that primarily comes from your inner child.

Did you know that 80% of your programming in your cellular body and DNA is downloaded into you by age 8? What does this all mean? It means most times when you are reacting to a life experience happening right now, you are feeling the pain and memory of similar experiences from your past, likely the Inner Child.

Authenticity is an act of loving self. It is not an act of a wimp, try it and see how much courage it takes to transcend the feelings of self-judgment. Love myself? What does that really mean? What is the connection between authenticity and loving myself? If I ask you to honestly tell me how you LOVE yourself, how would you answer that? You might say I love my self a lot. I give myself new clothing, massages, and trips. Awesome! Good for you. However, that does nothing to advance your true longing to manifest healing of pain, depression as well as healing of unhealthy relationships. You want a better life with inner peace, heartfelt joy, and greater abundance. Loving yourself with the items above only provides temporary comfort, which is where our ego comes in. The poor overworked ego works so hard running around like a medic on a battlefield providing bandages to cover up battle wounds. The ego works so damn hard to stop the bleeding, but alas it cannot. That was never the job of the ego. It was always the job of your heart to release painful programming and to manifest your dreams come true. To ask your ego to heal you is akin to asking your plumber to perform brain surgery. It is not qualified.

How does my heart heal me? My research and personal healing methodology has taught me that your brain is NOT your mind, so start using a tool that works well, your heart. Your heart is the new intuitive processing center for manifesting your life's experiences, dreams and manifestations. The heart creates a magnetic energy field up to 5000 times more powerful than the brain. If you need worthiness magnetic energy to manifest what you truly desire, then which organ will you use: Your Heart or Brain?

A good way to describe how one loves oneself would be to visualize a journey into a place of absolute worthiness that exists deep within every human cell and your DNA; to allow those feelings to be fully received with love and absorbed deeply into your cellular being. That place within you can be accessed in many ways, but most use meditation. There exists within you a place of absolute quiet, where attachment to time disappears and fear is absolved. It is the true divine makeup of each person. In this place, you will know and feel the love and the power of your own divinity. It is experiential. This Love and Power belongs to YOU, YOU, or YOU. Take your pick of any one of those three. When you surrender to your heart, knowing the intuitive energy that binds your subconscious mind to your conscious mind, you authentically love yourself. This intuitive energy is the secret to inspiration, to creation, to abundance, and living life in peace and harmony.

If you examined your current relationship to your life mate or your partner, you would see that at the core, there is only love. However, your ego has placed many conditional limitations upon that relationship based on your fears, insecurities, limitations, and judgments. Now, imagine yourself as an onion with multiple layers surrounding the core in the middle. Let's imagine at the core of the onion you are pure divine love and that all the outer layers represent your lower frequency thoughts, along with your beliefs of unworthiness. These lower frequency energies create gaps in communication styles and intimacy. They create failure or survival feelings that block you from fully receiving your partners love. Let's be clear, when it comes to your current unworthiness programming, please remember there is no judgment, nor have you done anything wrong, ever. We all have downloaded these limiting beliefs because we did not know any better. It is in fact part of your life journey (Karmic Blue Print). So, in relationship, the healing groundwork starts at a place of NO WRONG DOING. The healing potential of complete freedom from relationship killing beliefs exists, if you both choose to see it.

I recently wrote a book called, *Men, Sex and Food - Why Hearing A Woman Can Lead To A Deeper Love."* In this book I expose the gap that exists in men's beliefs around hearing their partner's feelings and the beliefs women have around clearly stating what they need from their man. Ultimately, a process is created to invite them both into a place of safety where the natural progression of what a woman needs in the venting process is honored and learned. This process requires authenticity, which leads to an opening for deep "IN TO ME SEE", intimacy. The results were deep intimate sex and a yummy meal, that got the man's attention.

The point being, that the way to a harmonious relationship is found in the re-programming of old outdated beliefs. Authenticity is the key catalyst. So, the connection between Authenticity, Healing, Loving Yourself, and Beliefs, is the potential for happiness, peace, and sacred union in relationship. The New and Improved YOU. Your dreams will come true by allowing yourself to talk the talk and walk the walk of living authentically. Authenticity is the, "Act of saying yes to claiming responsibility for your karmic, parental and societal programming, from a place of love, forgiveness and non-judgment."

When you open your heart to healing, you create measureable quantum energy healing opportunities.

Releasing these downloads of unworthiness creates an opening for new WORTHINESS information to be installed. This is also known as EMPOWERMENT. The words you speak, the feelings you feel, the thoughts you think, the beliefs you have programmed in your subconscious mind; all have a direct impact on your physical and mental well-being. Your relationships will thrive and your personal and workplace environments will feel harmonious.

Put the Law of Attraction to work for you effectively. If the Inner Child is in pain, heal the little boy or girl. Authenticity provides you with the keys to unlock the prison doors holding those old beliefs. This author had to do this work and I am very grateful for my freedom. You can do this, it is so freeing. I promise you great joy and inspiration as well. Your spirit, your heart, your mind, and your physical body will love you for it. Let your body feel so you can heal. What have you got to lose?

Rocky Krogfoss, President
New Beginnings Therapy Healing and Educational Services Global Healing Services via Distance Healing Stress Reduction Counselor, Life Coach, Quantum Energy Healer Vancouver, British Columbia, Canada
Phone: 604-510-0721
Email: stressfreeme99@gmail.com

Mari Mitchell

6 DISCOVERING THE MAJESTY IN ME

I was feeling so completely overwhelmed standing at my kitchen counter, that I was tempted to run out the back door just behind me and keep running. Never come back. What kept me standing there were my three children; a son who was ten and two daughters ages five and three.

No one had ever taught me how to love myself. In fact, I had learned just the opposite; do everything for everyone else with no concern for my needs or wants. Almost forty years of living my life in this fashion were catching up to me. I felt like I was on a merry-go-round that was going faster and faster, and I couldn't get off. I didn't have a nervous breakdown because honestly, "I didn't have time for one." Instead I just sucked it up, my life a series of unending tasks that neither gave me pleasure nor fulfillment. Of course there were moments of joy. My family was the source of most of that joy. I made sure that we had family time every weekend, so we went on outings, watched family movies, put on shows, and did all sorts of goofy things, mostly suggested from a book I had bought about family fun. That's when I felt like I was a good mother and my life was fine. Maybe I was just overreacting. But the next day, I would again feel overwhelmed, stressed, and see no way out of the unending responsibilities that were crushing me.

In church when we sang songs of praise, I felt peaceful and happy. But that quickly ended after the service was over and I returned to my "real" life: laundry, dishes, homework, volunteering at church, cooking, cleaning and running a part-time business for extra money. This along with arguments, whining, crying and nagging the kids and my husband to please help. There was no time for ME. Actually, there was no ME. I had morphed into who everyone else said I should be; an excellent mother, a faithful wife, a dedicated daughter, a good Christian. Why was I so unhappy and overwhelmed? I was doing all the right things, didn't God see that? I tried SO hard to please God and everyone else. I was a champion at Doing. It was Being I had no clue about, because I didn't even know who I was.

My first revelation came through a support group at church that dealt with co-dependency, a word I had never heard of. I joined the group and the weekly meetings gave me a glimpse into how much of a people-pleaser and perfectionist I had become. As the facilitator suggested, I began setting boundaries. I started with my mother. I knew that my mom loved me SO much, but she was also extremely dependent on me emotionally and physically. She didn't drive, so I drove her everywhere. She had no friends and I felt pressured to spend more time with her than I could spare in my already busy life, or even wanted to. As much as she loved me, she carried much fear and was extremely negative.

Setting boundaries with my mother was one of the hardest things I've ever had to do. I dealt with feelings of guilt and selfishness, feeling like a bad daughter. I forged on however, because somehow I knew deep down inside that this was the beginning of a better life. As I practiced setting more and more boundaries, I felt the wrath of my mother. She had no idea what was going on, only that I was changing and she wanted the old me back. I cried because I didn't want to be a bad person, I wanted to be good, to be liked, especially by my own mother. I stood firm in the boundaries I had set and eventually the guilty feelings eased and I felt proud of myself, but the next set of boundaries awaited. I knew I must take the next step, even if it meant going through all those guilty feelings again. To my surprise, it was getting easier. Now, it may seem that this was a quick and simple path. To the contrary, it took months and months to get to this point. This was just the beginning of my awakening to the fact that I deserved to be happy, fulfilled, and live in peace and tranquility.

The quest for ME unfortunately took me out of my marriage. After seventeen years, we separated then divorced three years later. As I started my new life as a single woman again, I was quite honestly thrilled. I felt free for the first time in almost two decades. My daughters came with me and my son stayed with his dad. I had gotten better at taking care of myself and my needs, but there was still so much to learn about loving myself. I still had that *Cinderella* story in my head that said if I found my "Prince," life would be perfect. So off I went in search of the man who would carry me away into the land of love and happiness.

Soon afterwards I fell in love, thinking this was the man I'd been waiting for and I gave him every part of my heart and soul. Six years later, I knew I must jump from the castle I had built with him, realizing he would NEVER bring me happiness. I loved him so much, but I was anxious, sad, worried, depressed, and frustrated most of the time. I felt both unloved and unworthy. I can try to blame him. I can blame society. I can blame my mother for reading *Cinderella* to me (actually, she never read to me, I read to myself). The truth is, I was looking for happiness outside of myself. I truly believed if I found the right man, the perfect job, achieved the perfect body, I would be happy.

I did some major work on myself in order to prepare to leave him and never go back. I journaled, listened to inspirational CD's, recited affirmations, read books, and slowly began to unearth the ME that was buried under piles of rules, *shoulds*, expectations, and beliefs that did not serve me. I started writing, feeling exhilarated as I shared the thoughts and ideas that had remained hidden inside me for so long. Every time I sat down to write, I felt fulfilled in a way I had never felt before and when members of the writer's group I belonged to actually said what I wrote was good, I was thrilled. I made new friends, reminding me how friendly and social I could be. I started connecting with myself and finding out what I liked and disliked, who I preferred to be around and what I enjoyed doing. Feeling better about myself, I was now able to write affirmations and ALMOST believe them. I am worthy. I am loved. I am beautiful. When I finally left him I was heartbroken, but I knew I had done the right thing and I was looking forward to building a happier and more fulfilling life.

Although I felt better with the burden of that relationship gone, I still lacked true inner peace and self-love. I was doing and saying all the right things, acting as if, as they say. But the actuality of stepping fully into the peace and self-love was yet to come. As I began to let go of people, beliefs and things that did not serve me, I experienced more peace and joy in my life. I was kinder with myself, slightly more patient and less demanding. I took time for baths with scented candles, read my favorite novels and got my hair and nails done. I joined several social groups and attended events, enjoying myself and making more friends. But, no matter where I went, or what I was doing, my radar was scanning the surrounding area for "Prince Charming."

It was a struggle to overcome all the years of programing I had undergone. Impatient with myself and others, I made my life a constant "beat the clock," always multitasking and getting everything done as quickly and as perfectly as possible. Stress was a constant, but I didn't realize I was the cause of that stress. I blamed my job, my boss, situations, and circumstance, but it was ME. It was the way I had created my life. I was always in my head trying to figure everything out and trying to control things so they would go my way and I could feel better. I didn't know that I could just choose to feel better regardless of the circumstances.

As I continued working on myself, I learned about Law of Attraction and that whatever I focus on, I bring into my life. I started testing the theory by focusing on parking spots. I would drive into a parking lot and visualize a spot right in front of where I was going. To my surprise and delight, it worked. I got so good at it that no matter where I went there was a parking spot available. Now parking spots are not that important in life, but this was the beginning of my being able to understand that I am in control of what happens in my life. I can create my own reality. I continued studying this Law, improving my ability to manifest what I wanted in my life. I was able to manifest a new amazing job, were I worked part time and earned full time pay, a gorgeous new blue convertible, and a lovely apartment overlooking downtown. I was on a roll. Now my life was truly becoming what I'd always wanted it to be, except for prince charming.

I decided to become a Life Coach and help others improve their lives, so I got my coaching certification. I started coaching part-time while still working my job. I couldn't wait to get out of work and do what I really loved. Prince Charming did arrive and I re-married in 2010. After talking with him about my desire to do my coaching full time, I left my job just before our wedding. I felt both deliriously happy and terrified. Although I had stepped into what I wanted, I had left a very good paying job to do so. I woke up in a panic each morning wondering how I was going to replace my salary with my new coaching business and if I didn't, what would my new husband say.

I'm not going to lie to you and say my business took off and money poured in from every corner of the Universe. It didn't. So I went into "Action Mode" doing everything a successful business woman is *supposed* to do. I did research on the internet and attended seminars. With my lovely notebook and pen in hand, I wrote down every suggestion, starred the ones I liked best, and began paving my road to business success. I attended networking meetings, met countless other business owners, gave out my cards, (which I had meticulously written to ensure the perfect copy) followed up with emails and calls, and waited for my clients to pour forth to me.

Nothing happened. Well, something happened. I did attract some new clients. Some wonderful clients who I love dearly and admire for the way they changed their lives. But the droves of new clients, they didn't appear. Two years I did this. I was back on that merry-go-round, but not in my personal life as much as in my business. I got up early, so I could look my best for whatever meeting I was to attend, barely getting in my quiet time. I hated going to those meetings. I just wanted to stay home and take time to connect with Source, Universe and myself. But duty called.

One summer morning in 2012 I was getting ready for a meeting and really didn't want to go. So I asked myself: "Why are you forcing yourself to go to this meeting? What about your Law of Attraction practice of reaching for what makes you feel good?" I wrestled with guilt, because I had volunteered to read the announcements that morning and I would be letting them down. Then I picked up my phone and called the leader of the group and left a voicemail saying I wouldn't be able to attend. Since I had made a commitment, I finished out my term and attended the next three monthly meetings. The leader was actually a bit cold towards me as I apologized for missing the previous meeting. I felt the hurt, then let it go, knowing I had done what was best for me, even if he was not okay with it. That was a turning point for me; choosing my own feelings over that of another, even in business, and feeling good about it. I had been doing it in my personal life for years, but had the mistaken belief that in business, you must sacrifice who you are and what you want, in order to get the clients. What a crazy belief that was! That was it. From that day on I decided to do what felt good for

ME in my business. That meant no more networking or anything else, unless I really felt drawn to it.

Then this expanded even more. Going to social events that I really wanted to attend, meeting with people I really wanted to meet with, calling someone I felt drawn to talk to. I also took a closer look at my personal life, realizing that even after so many years of practice, I was not consistently making the best choices for me. I made changes there also.

It did take courage for me to make these changes. Courage to stand by my decision to not meet with someone I didn't want to meet, (while being in fear of losing an opportunity for growing my business) courage to not go to the event EVERYONE else was going to because I felt deep down inside it wasn't for me, (wondering if I was making the right decision) courage to take time out for rest or fun while my ego was telling me I had too much work to do, courage to try something new because I felt deeply called to it, courage to walk away from people who kept me down with their negativity.

This led me to learning to truly trust myself and believe that I know better than everyone else what's best for me. That doesn't mean that I'm unteachable or unwilling to learn from others. It **does** mean that I must discern for myself what serves me and what doesn't. I've learned that the only way I know what's best for me is to FEEL it. I had to be willing to feel ALL my feelings, the bad feelings as well as the good and discern what they were telling me. Now feeling takes time, something I had given so freely to others, yet still had trouble giving to myself. Having been raised to do everything quickly and perfectly, I put many of my own needs aside in order to get the job done. I had a practice of quiet time for years, twenty or thirty minutes to get grounded and connect with

Universe/Source. But I was being called to more. I made a commitment to myself to set aside at least an hour every morning, (I call it my Sacred Space) and connect with Source, Universe, and ME. This is where I receive direction, inspiration, ideas; everything for my day. When I wake up I make my cup of coffee, then get into this space. This is essential for me and I don't skip it.

Practicing living this way has led me to be very kind to myself, because that's what my soul requires. Deciding to love myself enough by committing to do what's necessary for ME led to even more changes: no longer attending events out of obligation, taking a break during my workday, leaving work early or even taking the day off and doing something fun, taking weekends off, going to bed earlier, eating foods that fuel my body and give me energy and staying away from foods that make me lethargic or cause me to feel wound up. I still struggle with getting out and enjoying the outdoors, fresh air, and nature. That's something I'm working on and there might be some more self-love that needs to emerge in order for me to step into that fully.

Towards the end of 2014, I had a major revelation about myself. Actually it's about all of us. You included. I saw the Divine in me, the beauty and the splendor, the majesty. I was illuminated, expanded, and given a glimpse into a world of possibility, unlike anything I've even known. From this space is where I am living, creating, and expanding my life. I revel in the joy and love that is all around me and I am now to the point where I'm very sensitive to what I'm called to do, who I'm called to spend time with, and what I'm desiring to feel. I further felt called to invite others to experience this in their own lives, therefore I created a course called The Majesty in You, that will guide others to step into their majestic self.

My journey has been exciting and enlightening, as my eyes have been opened to the wonders of who I am and the greatness that surrounds me. And my journey continues, for I am excited to learn more ways to love myself, accept myself, and cherish who I am, my truth, my gifts, and all of me; to lift me up and in turn lift others, who perhaps cannot see the majesty of who they are – just yet.

My desire is that Your Majesty, the treasures that lay inside of you, will be revealed.

Mari Mitchell is a Certified Life and Relationship Coach, Author, Radio Show Host and founder of Dare to be Authentic ™and Preparing a Path to Love.™ She is also a Master Angel Card Reader offering guidance and encouragement. Her books include "*Diary of a Hopeless Romantic*", *Dare to be Authentic- Finding Your Authentic Self* and *The Cuban Heart.* She is available for speaking engagements and workshops. Her passion is helping people tap into the majesty inside of them, to create the life they desire. Contact her and she'll gift you your initial consultation.
Call: 954 243-7297
Email: mari@lifecoachmari.com
Website: http://lifecoachmari.com/

Penny M. Polokoff-Kreps

7 TELLING A DIFFERENT STORY

Looking back from where I am now, it is almost laughable that I spent so much of my life in a space of self-hatred, resistance, and misery. The plain, simple fact that I was a karmic being would have provided all of the answers that I needed to be at peace with myself. I took the longer, harder, route, the path less traveled, stopped to smell the roses, and got a lot of bee stings along the way. But, isn't that life?

My awakening took about forty years, with some times of real light and others of pervasive darkness that I thought would never end. At the same time, I always believed in some Utopia; a place where everyone loved each other and got along, worked in agreement with one another, and did not fight or exert power over anyone but themselves. As a little girl, I believed this as well, but lots of people told me it was ridiculous and stupid to believe that way and that I was crazy. I started to believe **their** truth and that's probably where the misalignment started, which caused me to create much negativity in my life.

My life had lots of high points and a few low points. I created a life that was guided more by suffering, isolation, feeling different, and being misaligned against the people that were to lead and teach me. I was an angry child, sought opportunities to fight, and was disruptive at home and school. I have no doubt that lots of people tried many ways to help me. I had to do it myself! This belief guided me through much of my childhood, into adolescence and young adulthood, where it really slapped me in the face. I had so many experiences that were fun while they lasted, but mostly risky, over-the-top, daring, and dangerous. I didn't care. I experimented and pushed the limits every chance I got. I loved to piss people off and make everyone else feel what I was feeling. I lived with a deep sense of wrath, a lot of aggression, and criticism which I integrated deeply, so that everything I experienced was through this filter. I spent most of my life feeling powerless, spiraling out of control, and in emotional pain. Whatever I was feeling seemed like it was the truth, for me. I believed my own stories and beat myself up mercilessly.

There were milestones in my life, "small hinges that swung big doors"; my high school teachers, in spite of my poor grades and emotional struggles, nominated me for a scholarship called the *Dr. Hannah K. Vuolo Citizenship & Leadership Award*, on the condition that I went to an out-of-state college. I accepted it. I excelled, loved learning, and did very well in my academics, but failed miserably in day to day life, unsure of myself, afraid of people, and not connecting with others in a meaningful way. I was emotionally immature and my coping skills were limited. It did not take long before I had to leave school, bordering on a nervous breakdown. My inner judgment of myself and the self-loathing came back in full force. I was still an excitement junky, struggling to live with any stability. I ended up in New York City gaining some life experiences, reading so many books, and working with a psychiatrist several days a week. Life was a mixed bag for sure, going to college part-time, working part-time in a bookstore, having my parents' support so that I could get back on my feet, and working in a soup kitchen with homeless people. I felt a calling to do social work, so I changed my major and began working toward my new career choice.

I got married at twenty-two, thinking it was a solution for my isolation. I found out really fast that I was ill equipped for intimacy. I was invisible in my marriage too. In five short years, the relationship ended. Over the time we were together, I had a car accident that required a long period of bed-rest and traction during which I became agoraphobic, leaving the house only for doctor's appointments and gaining over 100 pounds. I was miserable again. When the marriage ended I did what I always did: went to a 12-step program, enrolled myself in therapy, went on a diet, and "fixed" all of the things that were wrong with me. Almost as soon as I would feel "right" with myself again, having a sense of self-love, I would get into another relationship, shower my partner with all of my attention, and lose myself again. The next relationship was the game changer for my life.

I married again at thirty-three and immediately became pregnant with twins, after being told I would never have children. I had a strange sense that I would never fulfill my purpose. I was working in the City University of New York at the time, loving my job as a Career Specialist, helping people to find jobs, teaching a Job Search program that I wrote, and making a difference with my student clients. My life was very fulfilling. Four months into my pregnancy, I miscarried one baby and started to lose the other. It was necessary for me to go on bed-rest for six months and give up my career to keep my pregnancy. I went into a depressive rage for the duration. Wearing a belly-monitor and a catheter in my leg to stop the contractions, I did nothing but sleep, watch sad television shows, and cry. I was in and out of the hospital, needed to have surgery, and was afraid I would lose the baby. My husband was nurturing and kind. I was ungrateful and nasty.

I stayed home on disability until my daughter was five months old. I had always dreamed of being a mother, but never thought I would want to stay home. When I returned to work I was distracted and depressed, crying at my desk every day missing my baby. My doctor diagnosed me with severe post-partum depression. Struggling to choose between work and home, I had another car accident that made the decision for me; unconsciously I got what a wanted. However, after a while, being a mother felt as if it was not enough either. I obtained my first job as a freelance writer and worked from home, caring for my family and feeling more empowered than ever.

The happier I became with my own success, the more negative judgment I had for my husband. Somehow I now thought I deserved better. Just before my daughter's first birthday, I asked for a divorce. We separated. We went to court. Then months later after bitter fighting, we asked that our paperwork be withdrawn and we reconciled. We went to therapy and connected a little bit more successfully, but then returned to old patterns of neglect and anger. We packed up our lives and moved to Florida thinking it would make life easier, but in the back of my mind I knew it was already over.

A month after settling into our new home my father died. My father passing was another catalyst for my personal transformation. I grieved and grieved and grieved. I became aware of the fact that I had spent most of my life crying. I was a cry baby. I cried and cried and cried. It was just what I did. It was another familiar coping strategy for me just like over eating, raging, drinking, drugging, having sex. I could pervert anything and everything. My life was so out of control. I just could not see any value in my suffering. I was stuck in my life repeating the same cycle. I went back to 12-steps, therapy, and got another divorce. It's just what I did. Every time that something hurt me inside, I tried to fix it by making external changes. My thinking would change a little bit. I put my attention on the goal for a little while. But, once I achieved my goal of thin, calm, happy, successful, I would methodically destroy everything I had created and then do it again.

Once again, I could only see how ill-equipped I was at living and I hated myself some more. It was at this time, when my daughter was about five years old, I was screaming at her over something small and she looked up at me smiling and said, "Mommy, stop yelling at me. I love you." I heard her and for the first time in my life, I allowed myself to feel real love. I sat down on the floor with her in my arms and sobbed. She buried her little face in my neck and just kept kissing me. I remembered that when she was a baby and I was separated from her father, every time I cried, she would bring me a pacifier and stick it in my mouth, "all bettah now" she would say. This was love. I was feeling it through every cell in my body, like a fire burning within me, warming me in places that had been so neglected and misunderstood. I felt the part of me that was committed to destruction and hatred, as if there was a face-off between the forces of good and evil happening inside of me.

This time, I did not go on a diet or to therapy or to work. I stayed still. I focused on being a great mother. I lived off an inheritance. I did nothing but heal. I exercised and ate well. I made new friends. I met someone who was older than I was and had what I thought was going to be a brief experience, but as I began to evolve and my daughter was growing, I was experiencing something different. I was becoming aware of things I had never felt before. I had been happy, creative and in love before, but never really felt or appreciated it. Maybe turning forty was changing my perspective? Maybe I was catching up to myself and not having as much judgment? Maybe it was falling in love?

Once again, the unresolved and ill-equipped little girl started running the show and I started seeking answers outside of myself, looking for proof of my own existence. I started to feel exhausted and destroy my relationships. I started to feel lonely and overeat again. I began to blame my partner for my suffering, AGAIN. But this time something was different. I started to wake up! I started to notice that my behaviors were causing problems with my daughter's behavior. My extreme attitudes and inconsistencies were causing her to be afraid. She started developing symptoms of ADD and her needing attention got my attention.

We went to therapy together; my daughter, my boyfriend, and I. This was the first time that I had ever gone to therapy without any obvious drama of my own. We focused on how to support my daughter and I was given specific skills and actions to take that would help her be more successful in school and in life. I think the skills were meant for me to learn as much as her. As a family we were making strides and achieving success. We were all happy. I was ready to go back to work and loved my job. I started a business on the side and all was going well for a little while. My divorce was finalized and my boyfriend asked me to marry him. I said yes and scared the crap out of myself that I was going to get married a third time. I had to be crazy!

Now that I was living my bliss and loving my life, happier than I had ever been, the sabotage pattern was triggered again. I began to destroy what I had worked so hard to create. I knew I loved my daughter and my fiancé and I wanted the beautiful life we had. I also heard an inner voice telling me that I didn't deserve it. I was so negative inside. My self-hatred and self-absorption started to come back. Luckily, we were distracted by lots of fun and happy activities, buying a house, traveling, and had bonds to a community, so that when my bottom started to fall out again, there was a safety net.

My partner did not understand how much I was suffering because I showered him with love and attention, while beating myself up in silence. My daughter could tell and she would always ask me why I was so sad? I would just hug her and thank her for loving me while promising her that it would get better. When I was at work, busy and in the zone, it was all perfect. However, when I had nothing to do or had unscheduled time, I created drama; fighting with friends or family, overspending, overeating, anything to destroy myself. I fell into the old familiar habits, which were symptoms of the bigger problem and my unconscious compulsion for self-sabotage.

One morning I went to a networking meeting to promote my business and there was a woman there who offered "an operating manual to yourself if you were done with your suffering." I got her name and number and scheduled my first appointment. After an introduction to the Self Discovery Life Mastery process and having completed a "Personal Life Perspective," where I learned about Present Moment Awareness, I realized that I did not have to destroy anything else in my life. I could stop living life from the past or the future. I could be present in the moment and be able to choose what I really wanted. I could manage my emotions. This revelation was so powerful that I enrolled in the work and began a completely different journey with the support of a community that was committed to actualization, personal responsibility, and provided the discipline I had hungered for my whole life. I got to turn around and look at the life I had created up until then for what it was, a story. It was time to rewrite my story from an adult perspective. The childhood beliefs and strategies for survival no longer served me. This awareness brought liberation, a career change, a greater sense of purpose, and the words to say what I needed to say without hurting myself or others.

Looking back now, without the judgment and without the dark veil of negativity and suffering that I used to see my life through, I have come to love and respect myself and all of the earlier versions of myself, as having done the best I could. Learning to manage my emotions gave way to managing my consciousness, my thinking, and my feelings. I stopped operating on autopilot and started living deliberately. I started to feel the perfection of my life and accept that everything was the way it was meant to be. All of the information that I had inside of me from books I had read, to experiences I had earlier in my life and could not understand, seemed to make sense at a higher level and were integrated, so that I could FEEL it. I realized that all of the years of crying and denying what I felt so deeply and overwhelmed me, I had been resisting being myself. I had been keeping myself from my higher purpose. My journey was one of spiritual awakening and I began to see that my life was truly not just about me anymore.

I realized that all of the nightmares I had experienced both while awake and asleep, was a lifetime of shifting consciousness and just not knowing. The struggle and pain was necessary for me to experience my own version of soul awakening and transformation. Like a caterpillar in a cocoon, I was building strength, scratching through with all of my might to be reborn to myself and emerge a powerfully winged butterfly, taking flight in my life, soaring to my own highest heights, and going even further than I ever thought possible.

I can now easily value and appreciate myself for the journey I have created. Walking through my own psychic hell and now being on the other side, I can see value in every experience and have learned so many lessons, that all of it makes sense to me now. I am reminded of something my father once said to me when I was a teenager. He said, "life is like a mountain that you walk, spiraling around, raising in elevation with every step; and although you cannot see how far you have come, you can feel the change in atmosphere, and you can see more clearly and further away from where you are, on your way to the summit." I really appreciate his words as they explain so well what I was blind to until now.

It is so easy to buy into the drama and think that it's real, because it's what I see, but the path to self-love, to my own unique version of enlightenment, has been perfect for me. Through the eyes of love and non-judgment, I can see the inherent perfection in it all and I can extend forgiveness to myself at every level of existence that I did the very best I could with what I had. I extend this courtesy to everyone around me. I truly believe we are all doing the absolute best we can with what we have, in every single breath. With that in mind, this too is the very best that I can do here in this moment. It is my version of perfect. It is all that I am and all that I have to offer here. It is my version of love. I hope you like it. I finally do.

Penny (Penina) Polokoff is an accomplished Ghost Writer/Editor, Author of *Hero Woman, From Surviving to Thriving*, and *The Conversations Worth Having* series. She is a champion of many humanitarian causes, a noted public speaker, and has just added conflict resolution and mediation to her communications arsenal. She brings love, a bold commitment, and a stand for personal liberation to all of her projects. Penny can be reached for speaking, public performances, writer's workshops, and fundraising events via e-mail at: penwrites4u@hotmail.com

Joann Venezia

8 THE POWER OF ME

I'm writing from my home office in a quiet residential complex on the south shore of Long Island, New York. I love myself, my life, and feel very happy where I am. I have a wonderful son and an incredible husband. The business which I founded, YPI Consultants, is a business of empowerment, consisting of leadership development programs along with an institute. All this I created from a dream, a desire to be who I was meant to be.

It wasn't always this way. I had my challenges and I feel it is best to give you a view of my life so you can understand my journey. You may even feel your life is similar to mine. I remember a time when I didn't know what I wanted or needed to be happy and content. I wondered what it was like to be loved all the time. Not the unconditional love of a pet or the love from a parent, but the true deep love of another human being. I longed for a true sister, a brother or a friend who would be by my side and a man to accept me for who I am and to also accept and love my son.

I would ask myself, what is wrong with me? Why can't I just be loved and accepted for who I am? Why do people feel the need to hurt me, dismiss me or take advantage of me? I felt I was not loveable. But why? Did I really love me? Was I causing people to treat me this way? I needed to find the answers and stop the pain. I started to dig into my past to find out how this madness started.

During my elementary school years I was picked on for my last name, Dobrowolski, which they changed to "Double Bubble." My father had told me our name meant goodwill, which was a positive, so being picked on for my name was very confusing for me. To add to that, my attire was horrific, because it was hand me downs from my cousins. My sister being older, got the clothes while it was still fashionable, but by the time I got them they were well out of style. My *Johnny Appleseed* haircut and being overweight gave my classmates ammunition to pick on me and they did so in school and on the school bus. I vividly remember being on the bus to school one day, wearing an ugly yellow and black plaid dress with a pleated skirt, that was obviously from the fifties. Mind you, it was now the sixties and all the girls wore short dresses. Mine fell below the knee. I kneeled down on the seat and when I leaned forward the entire front of the dress ripped. I was mortified.

When I started junior high I found my voice and spoke my mind no matter the consequences. I did get into fights, but nothing major. My parents received calls from the school principal, but my dad always told us to stick up for ourselves. I remained strong, confident and just loved myself and believed in me for many years.

After graduating high school I went to secretarial school where I did well in the classes, graduated early and started working in Manhattan. Everything was going well. I met my first husband and I believed we would live happily ever after. The first three to four years we were best friends and all was well. Then things started to go wrong. At times the relationship was mentally abusive, other times verbal or even physically abusive. By the seventh year I knew it was over and I had to leave. When I finally decided to tell my husband I was leaving, I was terrified. I thought about leaving a note, but I knew it would be beneficial for me to tell him face to face. I will never forget that day, because when I was telling him I felt like I was six feet tall and he was four feet. I felt very powerful. When I think about that moment, twenty five years later, I can still feel that power.

Unfortunately, my second marriage was to a man who was verbally abusive and a cheater. We built an apartment onto my parent's house in order to better take care of them. When my son started realizing what was happening, I knew things had to change. My second husband had to go.

Much later I realized that after my first marriage, I was losing my edge, my smile, and my joy; my second marriage was no better. Being treated this way undermined my self-worth and destroyed a piece of me each time. It was a whirlwind of one storm after another coming at me. It is tough enough to have one abusive relationship, but to follow with a second makes it even harder to shift your mind in a better direction.

It was a scary time in my life. I had my son to worry about and I needed to keep food in his stomach, clothes on his back, and a roof over his head, not to mention mine. Yes, he had a father, but I needed to limit my exposure and time with him. All I worried about was my son. Then, just when my second marriage was ending, my son who was 16, decided to move in with his father because of all the arguing at home. The fights with my siblings who now lived in the same duplex as me and with my soon to be ex-husband took a toll on my son. He wanted peace in his life and I understood, but it was hard.

Shortly before my husband moved out, a family member moved in with my mother in order to help. My father was in a nursing home by this time and my mom was depressed. When my husband left I was horrified to become the object of this family member's abuse; a person who I had helped and supported in the past. Down again I went. How much more could I stand before I couldn't get up again? What did I ever do to deserve to be treated this way? I am a good person! I love my family and have given up my time with my child and husband to take care of them. I have even given up my vacation time to help them in times of need and yet, I am the one who gets abused, yelled at, called horrible names, and accused of stealing thousands of dollars. What did I do wrong?

When I decided to file an order of protection against him I had an eye opening moment. We had a conversation prior to the court hearing and he was able to convince me to dismiss the order and work on being a family again. When we discussed our decision with the judge, he blasted me for trying to bargain with the person who abused me, (typical behavior) saying that he was the one qualified to make the decision. After questioning the other party, the judge came to the conclusion that the order was to be enforced. WOW, were my eyes opened that day! I was truly surprised with the outcome. I was relieved, yet confused and afraid that I could have another repeat of the same situation. My mind, body, and soul could not handle it again. I was forced to face my fears, **no** face the truth. No longer could I pretend this was not happening. I was recommended by professionals who worked with these type of abusive situations, that I needed to get out of that home that was connected to my abuser's home. I would have to leave my mother and I had nowhere to go. It was a very hard decision to make, but necessary for my safety and sanity.

It was time for me to take a stand and decide what I wanted to do with my life. I was alone, no husband, no child, (living with me) and now no home or family who cared, except for my parents. I told my mother I would be in contact with her when I was able and I did. I always loved and cared for my parents. They would do anything for me and I for them. We had the unspoken promise. However, it was time for deep down soul searching and getting my life in order. I never felt so scared or alone in my life. All I had was my car, what I could pack inside of it, and barely any money. The couple of hundred I had saved to use for an apartment was withdrawn from my bank, because I had neglected to listen to my inner voice and close the account. My checking account was so negative it would take months to save enough to get my own apartment. All I kept thinking was, they may have my money, my son, the house, and think they are winning, but they do not have ME!

A friend was kind enough to open her home to me however, her husband reminded me too much of my first husband and staying there was uncomfortable. After a month I was offered a roof over my head in exchange for house sitting. Since the house was on the market, I had to leave during the day and wasn't allowed to use any dressers or closets, having to take all my belongings with me every day. After four weeks of living this way, I found a tiny little cottage on a canal, with no insulation and gaps in the wall. It was ice cold, but since it was behind the main house and far from the road, I felt safe. No one could find me. My piece of heaven.

What needed to change so I could find peace? Why were these events repeating? Why did only men abuse me, or did I only let men abuse me? Why these men and no other men in my life? What was I doing to get them in a state of abuse? So many questions and I had no answers. More questions bombarded my mind. What do I do to stop it from happening? Where do I turn? And the most important question, who can I trust to help me? Most of us have asked ourselves, what did I do wrong? If you think long enough, you probably could come up with several answers and keep the finger pointed right back in your face. But that will not help you, it will keep you right where you are.

I was so frustrated with myself. It seemed no matter how hard I tried to get away or stop the madness, it always found me. I needed to figure out how to save myself and quickly before something else happened that I might not be able to restore myself from. Thankfully, I had my faith to keep me going, give me peace, and keep me focused. I also had a full time job which helped me a great deal. I would go to work every day focused on my job and not let my life interfere. It gave my mind a rest for those hours when I was busy. When I was not, I had to keep my mind focused and not cry or show my fears.

I quickly learned that I needed more money to get where I wanted to be. I tried getting a second job within the mall I was working, but it was a conflict of interest. My current job came with a base salary plus commission from sales. My options were to find a new job, or make more money where I currently worked. I needed to look at what I had to offer to either a new employer or my current manager and see how I could make it all work in my favor. I had to look within me, discover what I was capable of and stretch myself outside of my comfort zone. How would I apply for a job without having an address? That was just one of my problems. I had to start moving forward, but I was very scared. What would happen to me? Where would I live? What if I screwed up so badly that I lost my job?

All the negative conversations in my head had to stop as I re-focused on the results I needed and more importantly, I wanted. That ability to remain focused on creating the ideal situation for me is what I believe moved me along. Life was teaching me a lesson. It showed me who I am and what I can accomplish if I put my mind to it. I had to work every day on me. It was not easy, but it sure was worth it. I had to dig deep within me to find the true me. On the outside, you would not know what was happening inside. I didn't take my problems to work, I wanted it to be a *no problem zone*. That separation was one way for me to feel free and at peace. A sense of accomplishment, I told myself. When I saw happy people,, I imagined myself living that way with my family and friends. Missing that connection in my life I would cry, feel rejected, unworthy, and think it was not possible for me. Maybe I'm not meant to be loved. Am I supposed to be alone? That was not the life I imagined at all.

I learned so much about myself. I discovered **not** to let others speak for me or tell me what I needed to do. I learned to listen to my inner voice, it was speaking to me for a reason. If I would have listened to what my inner voice was telling me sooner, I would have a different story to tell. That is a lesson I chose to learn the hard way. I did research at the library to learn how to help myself. I read a lot of self-help books, articles on the internet, and kept looking at what I wanted. I would monitor how things were changing for me and how I responded to key people in my life, positive and negative. I had to remove the negative and hurtful people. I had to take a look at who my friends were. Did I really have any? What common traits did these people have and what impact did it have on me? I started to notice that I was gaining my self-worth again.

What was more interesting, I noticed those other people had a lack of confidence. Some of them actually stopped speaking to me as I moved closer and closer to being myself. I learned that the people you associate with have a big impact on your life. If you hang around individuals with low self-esteem, your self-esteem will suffer. You may not notice it at first, but it will have an impact on you and your life. I removed as much negative or bad influence as I could. If I had to associate with those type of people, I kept my distance and made sure that conversation was simple with no details. I also made it a point to go and touch the things I wanted, material things, to connect and bring these items closer to my reality.

So, what has changed for me? I am now focused on what I want in my life. I have decided that my life is to be written by me and I fill in the blanks. I had to learn who I am. I needed to know why I react the way I do in different situations. I had to get *naked in the mirror* and take a good hard look and remind myself that God Does Not Create Junk, that I am as capable as I allow myself to be! It is not what others think of you that matters. It is what you think, believe and tell yourself that matters the most. We all are given gifts and talents when we are born. They are part of us and when we allow others to tell us who we are, what we are capable of, and how worthy we are, we give our personal power away. Usually, those individuals who are trying to dictate our self-worth have little themselves and have more issues then we do.

My advice, *get naked in the mirror*. Love and accept yourself for who you are right now. Never let anyone else dictate your life or even a page of your life story. Test yourself from time to time and step outside your box and meet the challenge that is waiting for you around the corner. Start to see who you truly are and what you are made of. Hold on to your personal power and let others see it. Let them experience your personal power and watch what happens. I guarantee you will be surprised.

From time to time I am sugar and spice and everything nice. Other times, I am determination, cause and effect with a little bit of history that reminds me who I am; a Child of God, who does not create junk! As for keeping away from the abusive and negative individuals, I am now equipped with an internal alarm that tells me when I am dealing with that type of personality. I have the tools I need to move away from them and stay at a distance. I was able to seek out the help and counsel I needed to move forward.

Life teaches us lessons every day and every day we need to keep our minds open to new ideas and accept change for what it is, not what we want it to be. Learn to breath and enjoy every day you are given. Stay focused on your goals and keep your dreams alive. If you do not give them life, who will? Never underestimate the *Power of You*!

Joann Venezia, is the Founder and President of YPI Consultants, LLC, a corporate efficiency and leadership development company. Joann lives her passion through YPI Consultants where she Empowers, Educates, and Motivates Organizations for success. She works with CEO's, HR professionals and entire teams. By offering the most comprehensive and innovative tools available, she deliver effective and customizable solutions for the recognition, understanding and development of human potential.

Phone: 631-320-0217
Email: j.venezia@ypiconsultants.com
Website: www.ypiconsultants.com

J. Daniel Gawrys

9 MY BETTER LIFE STORY

My earliest memory of heartbreak was when I carved my name into the front window sill of my childhood home. My mother had just told me that she and my father were getting a divorce. I was five years old when my definition of family was shattered. At that moment, I learned that my heroes, mentors, and first teachers didn't love each other. I can still feel the pocket knife in my hand and smell the paint scoured by each cut, as the wood softened against my blade. My heart broke and all the pieces lay within each letter I carved into that window. Metaphorically I was asking for help: "I am here, I am hurt, my family needs help, this is my home, I belong here, please don't take me away."

At that time my father worked hard and played hard. My mother found comfort in food. My parents argued and yelled, keeping me and my two younger brothers up late at night. I felt scared and unsafe, so I went inside my mind to hide. I clenched my teeth and fists, angry at my mother and father for not loving each other. I covered my gentle heart in armor to keep it safe. Although photographs of me as a young boy show a smile on my face, a saddened frown lay within my heart. Longing for relief from the deep emotional pain that lay silently inside, the question of why I didn't die from heart break early in my life can only be answered by the invitation to share my story with you.

A BETTER WORLD

As the oldest of three brothers, I adapted a pattern of self-reliance to make sure I could take over caring for my brothers, if necessary. Our parents, who had their own problems, didn't seem to be aware of the impact their relationship was having on us. I was good at keeping secrets. No one knew what I thought, how I felt, and especially that I didn't trust people, including my own parents. I felt that at any moment our life as a family would end; somehow it lasted twelve more years.

I thought that somehow God made a mistake. I should've been born in another place and time. I felt insecure, unsafe, and unworthy of being alive. As a teenager I frequently thought of running away. I rode my bicycle every day because it made me feel free from the emotional pain. Several times I took a solo forty mile roundtrip bicycle ride from our home to Duxbury Beach. We went there as a family during the summertime, had fun, and were happy together. Riding my bicycle to the beach made me feel connected to my family and to the real world outside. I knew there was a better life and was determined to find it no matter how far I had to go.

I loved climbing to the top of the trees. I would perch myself on the highest branch, close my eyes, and listen to the leaves wrestling in the wind. I would sit up there for hours, creating a better life story for myself. The wind set the tone for a better life as it carried the aroma from the lilac bush below, up to the tree tops to greet me. I still remember the smell of the late spring breeze and the feeling of wind kissing my cheeks. I loved being outdoors, feeling grounded, exploring the world, and feeling connected to it.

In grammar school I loved when our librarian read us stories acting out each character. In my last year, I tested very high in reading, writing, and literature and was placed in the advanced writing class for the new school year. I was confused by one of my assignments, but didn't ask for help just doing the best I could. My teacher told me, right in class, that I was stupid and would never achieve anything in my life because I didn't have what it took to be functioning at such a high level. She didn't know that I was never exposed to the curriculum leading to that assignment, because I had tested out of and skipped that level the year before. My teacher yelled, belittled, and embarrassed me that day and it stuck with me. My credibility was at risk from that point on and I was determined not to feel that way ever again. Although I always worried what people thought about me, I acted like I didn't care.

A CHANGE IN PERSPECTIVE

I often visited my father at work when he was the supervisor of the housekeeping department in a community hospital. I was very impressed by the healthcare workers and their commitment to helping people. He started working there when he was in high school and was re-hired after he returned from

Vietnam. A Marine Corps Vietnam War combat veteran, my dad was very sick with colitis. Several years after coming home he met my mom, they married, and I was born. I grew up watching war movies with my dad after he drank a few too many beers. The agony, pain, and tears I saw on his face, along with his screams of "get out of there it's a booby trap," scared the hell out of me.

My mom's sister had her own war stories about how my mom and her other siblings were disciplined as children. There was unspoken sadness and grief in my home. I loved my family so much and wanted to help them but I didn't know how.

My father frequently pushed himself beyond his limits. He made sacrifices all his life; as a boy who needed to act as a man while his father was away at war, as a soldier for his country, and then for his own family. He empowered my brothers and me to do our best and taught us that there is no wrong or right, just different perspectives. He volunteered at a local Catholic church. He often worked double shifts at the hospital to bring in enough money. My dad had trouble saying no when someone asked for his help, even if it meant impacting him in a negative way. He was dedicated to serving people because this was his calling. He worked very hard in and outside the office, never resting. Although I was concerned about his overuse of alcohol, he stopped drinking when I was an early adult. In those years my dad was laid off from his job, put himself through college, earned a business degree, and reestablished himself as a business professional with a new career in finance. He demonstrated that overcoming obstacles took hard work.

My portrayal of being in control and happy on the outside was a cover up for not dealing with my own feelings. I always felt like I needed to be strong for other people, so I hid my emotions. I was sensitive to others and had lots of empathy because I knew no matter what it appeared to look like on the outside, everyone was dealing with something on the inside. I wanted to help, to listen, and most of all learn how to control situations in my own life so I could be like my dad and be of service to others.

SEPARATION

My parent's lack of communication inspired me to learn how to cope with conflict and be a better communicator. I found so much joy and comfort expressing myself through sports, acting, singing, and dancing on stage in high school and throughout college. When I was performing, I could be whoever I wanted to be.

In junior college I studied social work and psychology because I wanted to fix myself. I learned how to express myself, to ask questions with empathy, and not to judge people for the negative things that had occurred in their life. I developed very close relationships with both of my grandmothers in order to complete a genealogy assignment. I asked challenging questions that were difficult for my grandmothers to answer and learned the root causes of why my parents triggered each other in a negative way. I empathized with my family and understood them as people who made the best decisions they could. I learned that cardiovascular disease was prevalent on both sides of my family. This led me to making health and wellness a priority in my life.

I chose a career in healthcare to teach and help others. My first official career job in a hospital was in Cardiology as a Cardiac Sonographer where I used ultrasound medical imaging to see how patients' hearts functioned. I found my passion in my work clinically and later shifted to the business side of healthcare where I used technology to help people from a global perspective. I created and implemented innovative cutting edge solutions; mentored, coached and taught healthcare providers how to use tools to improve patient outcomes.

As I traveled for business and worked seventy plus hours/week, I learned the world was much bigger than I thought and all people have the same needs. I learned about managing stress by becoming burned-out. I worked and played hard and reminded myself of my dad. I was very dedicated to my work but felt like I created obstacles that impeded my personal success.

I was forced to reexamine my life after I got laid off from the company I dedicated my life to during the early 2000's. A year had passed since my fiancé and I relocated from New England to North Carolina where we had built a house with dreams of creating a family. My life turned upside down that day in October 2008 when I was told my job was eliminated. Two days later my fiancé was laid off from her job. The real estate bubble had burst and the economy was crashing. I didn't know what to do, so I got back on my bicycle looking for answers. The answer came on a mountain bike ride. I pushed myself beyond my limit that day as I attempted to defeat every summit I encountered along those trails. I found myself defeated as I became suspended in air wondering if this was how my life was going to end. As I flew over the handle bars, my body launched into a momentous tumble down a hill catching every protruding rock and root from the trees that lined the trails. After I stopped rolling down the hill, I lay there for a moment wondering if I was dead. I used every ounce of mental, physical, and emotional energy to dust myself off and get back on my feet. Battered and bruised from life's greatest lessons, at that moment I realized I had become separated - in my life, in my work, and especially in my right shoulder from that crash.

One separation led to another. My fiancé and I separated ourselves from all the possessions we held on to for so many years. We sold nearly everything we owned, let go of our dreams, including the house, as we prepared to move back home. During the preparation phase I was introduced to chiropractic medicine as a way of healing from my shoulder injury. I learned about several integrative healing practices such as movement, meditation, prayer, music, acupuncture, chiropractic medicine, massage therapy, and connecting with nature.

A year later, after returning to Boston, I developed excruciating facial pain and was diagnosed with trans mandibular joint dysfunction. Years of built up stress, clenching my jaw, grinding my teeth, and the layered injuries from the mountain bike crash, led to the realization that I had not taken care of myself. I remembered what I learned from my Chiropractor in Charlotte and began seeing another Chiropractor in Boston. He said my body was telling me that I needed to change something in my life. I began my own stress management regimen and practiced on a regular basis. Through my deeper sense of self-awareness, I began to notice that in my personal life I lived one way and in my professional life I lived another. I worked so hard in my career that my personal life had become imbalanced. The stress in my life had negatively impacted all my relationships in and outside of work.

The calling for living in positive relationships

became louder and louder over several years of losing people that I loved so dearly, especially my grandmothers. Death became my inspiration for living a life of more meaning. I began my own personal journey to find that in my life.

Upon returning to Boston my fiancé and I married. We worked very hard to support each other's work and dreams. After the tenth time of my wife telling me to follow my own dreams, I finally listened. I was afraid that if I did seek out my own dreams, it would mean a probable end to my marriage and I was right. Although we had been together for twelve years and supported each other through many life transitions, we knew in our hearts this was not our path. We loved each other so much that we needed to let go, so we could each grow on our own. I had always felt that she and I were meant to be together as teachers along our journeys, but now I had realized it was time to move on. I was afraid to let go, because the experience brought back all the emotional trauma of being a child of divorce. This invited me to learn who I really was, rather than to remain that scared little boy who had been hiding for so many years. My separation and divorce from my best friend was the most difficult thing I had ever done in my entire life. I am thankful that we worked through it together.

THE CONTINUED JOURNEY

One day, I was fortunate to be at the right place at the right time when I met a business professional at a local entrepreneur event. I accepted his invitation to a free professional development seminar. Three days later I was in a classroom and heard words that I always felt in my heart but never had the courage to say out loud. At thirty-eight years old I began a journey of self-discovery and life transformation with the support of two people I met at the Center for Phenomenological Leadership in Pawtucket, RI. who became my mentors. That year I learned how to recreate my self-identity and to tell my story of who I was and who I wanted to be. Reframing my self-perspective and the life events that occurred in my past, gave me the ability to see my life as it really was, a gift. My mentors coached me using tools such as writing and journaling. The scattered ideas, thoughts, emotions, and perceptions I had of my inner world began to take form and heal my broken heart. As I became more organized in my thinking, my emotions began to follow. I improved my leadership skills and got promoted at work. I expressed myself creatively at work and more effectively in my relationships both personal and professional.

Because of this transformational experience, I wanted to do work that was more meaningful. For a year I was able to create more meaning in my work by using my desire to promote cardiovascular health and use it as a catalyst to create a wellness culture for the company I worked for. I realized that I had been given an opportunity to trace back to the past, pick up all the pieces of my broken heart and put them back together again. In order to continue my transformational journey outside of work, with the support of my mentors, I applied for graduate school at Saybrook University and was accepted.

Through my continued learning, I was able to connect with my dad from a much deeper level. I learned that he had post-traumatic stress from his experience in the Vietnam War. Sharing his story with me deepened our relationship. This helped me gain more empathy and patience for other people. My life suddenly began to make sense as I learned how his trauma and PTSD from the war had impacted his life and mine. As my life began to transform, I re-interpreted my past story and allowed the scared little boy inside me to begin to heal even more. I followed my dream of living in a place where I could experience summertime all year long, moving to San Diego, California where my dad was born. I learned that relationships provide opportunities to learn from our collective experiences and that patterns in life continue to repeat, until we pay attention to what we are supposed to learn. Once we are able to focus our attention, our duty is to embrace what we've learned, apply it, let go, and then teach others.

MAKE EVERY ACT AN ACT OF LOVE

Until a year ago, when I felt lost, I disconnected from my relationships to go deep within myself to reconnect. When I looked into the shadow bag of all the perceived negative experiences that I collected to define my life, what I found was a wealth of teachable moments that formed who I am. I've become whole again through focusing on positive relationships, personal and professional development, and learning that my life journey and passions stem from working to heal myself from my parent's divorce. I consider myself a student of life and now know that God didn't make a mistake when I was born. I know that I am here to help other people heal and discover their own truth. I have made a commitment to myself to live only in healthy relationships. Every day I wake up and I dare myself to be authentic. I invite you to join me in practicing to make every act an act of love and to create a better life story.

Daniel is the CEO of Viscosity Solutions "Adaptable Performance Leadership with Heart" The company provides professional development through customized programming online and offline, live traditional retreat based, innovative distance learning programs, business coaching for executives, mid-managers, and teams, as well as an executive leadership coaching practice. They believe professional development is an inside (about you) outside (about your role) job; it's about you first and the role you play second.

Daniel is also a graduate student studying Integrative Medicine at Saybrook University. His research interest is the physiological mechanisms of mental performance and stress.

Direct Line: (858) 707-5604
www.viscosityconsulting.com
https://twitter.com/viscositysolutn
https://www.linkedin.com/in/jdanielgawrys

Debbie Perkins

10 TRANSFORMED BY UNCONDITIONAL LOVE

They say hindsight is always 20/20 and as I have written my story, I have come to realize that the life experiences I have been through have brought me to a place of self-love. This was my path to discovering who I was and ultimately led me to love myself.

I grew up with parents who were very abusive to each other. My Mom and Dad's hate for one another was what I thought was normal and the way every family acted and reacted to each other. They never sheltered me or protected me from anything. I learned at a very young age to lie about all our family secrets. The constant deceit and dishonesty from my family destroyed my self-esteem. This led me to become a care taker and I spent most of my life taking care of others, but I always neglecting myself.

I started sneaking around and smoking cigarettes with my siblings when I was six years old. We learned quickly how to get away with it and not get caught. Even from my early childhood I felt bad about who I was inside, because I was molested by a family friend who gave me alcohol. In order to keep myself from feeling bad, I became a drug addict. This way I did not have to feel at all. My life was good as long as I could stay out of my head and not deal with what was going on around me. As a result, I spent most of my life in active addiction. Throughout my adult life it was constant trauma and turmoil; from domestic abuse, to both my parents committing suicide, to my being raped, followed by several felony arrests, and three prison terms due to my drug addiction.

I was a Cosmetologist for many years and my goal was to buy a salon and do hair for the rest of my life. I never really had dreams and goals for myself other than that, because I was always relapsing and going back into the same destruction. At the age of forty-six I did not have a clue who I was or what I was going to do with my life. I had so many old tapes in my head that told me over and over again that I was unworthy, unloved, and this is just what I deserved because of all the bad things I did to myself and others. Thoughts about bad decisions were constantly flooding my mind bringing with them feelings of self-loathing and guilt. By the time I became sober, I had absolutely no idea about the person I was or who I wanted to become. I had a lot of work ahead of me in order to stay sober and learn all those values I was deprived of growing up. It's one thing to get sober, but to stay sober I had to deal with all the damage and pain, not only that I had lived through, but that I had caused.

At the beginning I kept making mistakes with all the old habits because I was really good at deceiving people to get what I wanted. When I lied to someone, I didn't feel good inside and thoughts of using would always follow, because using would make me numb to the guilt. All these feelings were new to me because while in active addiction I did not have to feel at all. I didn't give up and I kept improving, day by day and that's when I started feeling better about myself from the inside. I was taught in a 12 step program that I could not stay sober alone, but that we could do it together. I started sponsoring women in the program and in helping others I began feeling really good about changing my ways and how I now treated others.

There is no perfect in my life and in the beginning I found myself saying I was sorry to someone every day, because of the way I was used to treating people. I could not lay my head on my pillow until I did. As I practiced more and more treating people better, the old habits seemed for the most part to stop. I had to learn how to change all the old habits that would make me feel bad on the inside. I would always have this little voice in my head that would tell me not to do whatever I was about to do, yet I would never take heed ending up right back in the insanity of active addiction. I learned how to put my recovery first and that's when my outlook on life started to change. I learned how to listen to that voice inside of me that would guide me in the right direction, which I now know was God helping to change my future. This helped me to start feeling proud of myself and the decisions that I made on a daily basis. In recovery, I learned that it is a daily reprieve and it was up to me to deal with my past so that I had a chance at a future. Day by day, I started feeling better on the inside and being very proud of who I was becoming, my self-love was emerging.

After my last arrest I was put on two years house arrest. I of course had a lot of time on my hands and conveniently my neighbor asked me if I wanted a horse. I figured it couldn't hurt and would give me something to do. Well, I had no clue when they brought the horse over early that morning that he was next to dead. It was freezing cold that day and I had walked out to make sure the gate was latched wearing shorts and flip flops. When I realized the horse was flat on the ground, I knew he was in trouble. He had colic, a belly full of dirt, and only wanted to lie down and die. I forced him to get up and walk. So many times in my life I wanted to lie down and die, so I knew exactly how he felt. I was not going let him die! I walked him for twenty-three hours straight with no time to change into warmer clothes and shoes. Every time he lay down again, I was screaming and crying at him, "I want to lie down too. You've got to get up and keep trying. Now is not the time to give up." Possums and raccoons were everywhere, but I kept them away with a big stick all through the night. My determination to save this horse got me through. By the time the sun started to rise I could see new life in his eyes, he now had the will to live.

I felt that what happed to this horse was exactly what had happened to me. Up to when I was seven, my mom was always trying to protect herself from my dad. She was unable to give me the love and care I needed, so I was just like that horse eating dirt. From the age of three or four I began protecting her and my other siblings.

It took six months to nurse my horse Paul back to health. During this time I was living with my step-dad and was taking care of him since he was dying from cancer. I didn't want to cry in front of my dad, so I would go outside to spend time with my horse and he would lay his head on my shoulder as I cried, as if he knew my pain. I felt unconditional love from Paul. This opened me up to receive and give love. After having Paul for over three years he reverted back to the racehorse he was born to be and I knew in my heart that he needed room to run. While he taught me how to become free of my past, it was time to set him free. Paul now resides in Jupiter, Florida on 120 acres where he can run free.

I now wanted what everyone else had, marriage and the white picket fence, but it was never going to happen until I learned how to forgive and be forgiven. I started listening to the suggestions that were given to me. It was a very painful process because of everything that I went through and never dealt with. For the first year of my sobriety I stayed away from men. That is when I really searched for who I was and what I wanted to do with the rest of my life. I started digging deeper and getting to know a person that I really never knew before, ME!

When I really started working on myself in the 12-step program I started to change. I had to learn how to change all the behaviors that I learned throughout my addiction. Habits like lying, cheating, and stealing, because I could never feel good about myself while doing those things. I had to listen to what was going on in my head and discern my addict mentality versus reality. My addict mentality would tell me that it's okay to tell a little white lie or to steal something and no one would know. My addict mentality would tell me that I am doing really good or really bad and it would be okay to use just one time and then go back to my life. But the true reality is, if you use once you will never stop. As I stopped listening to the voice of the addict my life took on new meaning and I actually started to have a real life.

I have had a lot of death in my life and always stayed high so I wouldn't have to deal with any of it. While taking care of my step dad who was dying of cancer, I realized that just because I was sober did not mean life was going to be easy. The love that I had for him was unconditional and I was given the opportunity to give him all my love and care that he so desperately deserved. Doing this helped me to learn how to love myself, just as when I had nurtured my horse to health and to learn how to feel proud of what God had put in my path in spite of the pain I had gone through.

I had always felt that I had to be in a relationship to feel good about me. I was always searching for a perfect relationship, one that I would feel safe in and loved for the person that I was. I was always told when I would try to get sober, to stay out of relationships, but I would never listen. I always felt like I had to have a man in my life. Every time, I picked men who were just like my father, very abusive. I mean most of us grow up and become like the people who raised us. I had no self-esteem or self-worth so searching for that perfect relationship was never going to happen, until I learned to love me. Since I did not love myself I would pick men who were not capable of giving me what I deserved. I didn't believe I deserved to be loved. How could I pick a healthy relationship when I wasn't healthy mentally or spiritually?

In the 12 step program they teach you to stay in the day and do the best you can with what happens in that day. Well, I kept telling my story over and over because it seemed I was always meeting people who were in the same kind of pain that I spent most of my life in and I could give them hope, because let's face it, if I can get and stay sober anyone can. That's when I started to realize how helping others was a way of helping myself. I kept praying and asking God to guide my day and help me find my purpose. I began getting on my knees every morning and asking GOD to help me to help someone else. I tried to become selfless instead of selfish and my whole outlook on life changed. I learned to stay by myself and how to love unconditionally from the inside.

While I was taking care of my dad who was dying, I met a man in a meeting who helped me to get through my dad's illness and his passing away. I can say that was truly the first healthy relationship I had ever been in. One month after my dad passed away my boyfriend was diagnosed with stage four throat cancer and my first thought was to say, "the hell with it," and go back to what I had always known, getting high and not dealing with any of this at all. Well, to my surprise, my spirituality kicked in and I did not run. I faced it head on with my faith in my God who I knew would get me through. In doing so I learned to depend and have faith in God's understanding and not so much my own understanding of why things continued to happen to me. I tried to stay out of the "poor little old me" mentality and just stay in the "one day at a time" mentality. What I know is that I cannot control what happens, but I can control how I deal with it. This allowed me to take care of my boyfriend the best way I knew how, with love. I felt very proud of me, my behaviors and how I handled myself in spite of all the pain I was constantly in. It was then and there when my true self-love started to manifest.

When my dad passed away he left the house to me, my daughter and sister, with the requirement that my daughter and I keep possession of the house for five years and it could not be sold. On my limited income, I couldn't afford to stay in the house. A friend of mine suggested I turn it into a half-way house for recovering addicts and alcoholics. The last thing I wanted to do was deal with a bunch of drunks and drugs addicts! After thinking about her suggestion, I realized it was my only choice in order to keep the house, it just made sense. So I started getting women, one by one and while working so closely with them it became my passion in life. Day by day I realized God's plan for me. By learning how to give back and do what I do in my life for the right reasons, my love for others and myself grew.

My journey through self-discovery has been a very difficult one. I realize now that it was all necessary in order for me to learn who I was and where I was going. I'm now a nationally certified interventionist, life coach, anger management coach, recovery coach, sober coach, and working on my Masters addictions coaching certification with Cali Estes out of Miami. I am also the owner of one female transition house and three male transition houses, with a total of sixty-six beds. When I founded these houses I made sure they were all pet friendly, because my animals have been a huge part in helping me to heal and to love again. Most of my clients are now doing equine therapy at Angel's Recovery in Wellington Florida, which is teaching them trust, self-discovery, and self-love. All the things I learned in my caring for Paul, my step-dad and my boyfriend.

All my life I was held hostage because of the trauma that happened to me. What I know today is that GOD had his hands on me throughout my entire addiction and I was never really alone. I'm now living out his master plan. I am now capable of giving and receiving love unconditionally. Let go of your past, forgive others, and mainly forgive yourself. Learn to live freely and believe that God has a plan for you.

Debbie Perkins is a nationally certified interventionist, anger management coach, life coach, recovery coach, as well as a sober coach. She is also the owner of Acme Ranches Transition Houses located in Wellington, West Palm Beach and Lake Clarke Shores.
Phone 561 880 7877

Kathleen Stroman

11 LOVE THROUGH THE
JOURNEY OF AUTISM

Being a parent of two children with autism spectrum disorder (ASD) rips your life open so very wide, that every vulnerable part of you automatically becomes exposed to the world. I had no choice, no learning curve, or an Autism for Dummies book. As a parent I became adept at calming my children and quickly handling the meltdowns, operating on hyper vigilant anxiety to protect them from anyone and anything that could attempt to capitalize on their sensitivities and fragileness.

My two children, particularly my youngest, are extraordinarily sensitive, as many on the spectrum are. Call it what you want "autism," "autistic," "non-neuro-typical"; there is huge debate in society over this. My youngest son senses and reacts intuitively to sounds, temperatures, weather, astrological events, full moons, scents, chemicals, movements, other people's energy, along with voices, vibrations, colors, lighting, and immensely to electromagnetic energy (EMF) such as computers, cell phones, smart meters, microwaves, and televisions.

This exceptional intelligence makes it very difficult for him in our chaotic, obsessed, and ego driven world. So many people are stressed out, depressed, and frenetically scurrying through life in an overwhelming confusion of daily activity. The intensity of all this emotional unpredictability and confusion is immeasurably felt by my sons, but not fully validated by scientific evidence, so it is not actively discussed or a huge concern in our schools and everyday life. In fact, just writing about this most likely categorizes me as crazy, bizarre, and witch like. Put me in whatever category you want, I know my children are wired differently and that is okay.

Taking my youngest to many public places is most certain to cause a reaction with the overabundance of incoming stimuli. How could it not? He is overly empathetic to the world around him, something I can't change. The sudden onslaught of whatever he is feeling, hearing, or sensing can cause an abrupt shift that lunges him into full on "meltdown" mode. These "meltdowns" are not pretty and there is no way to describe the intensity. Times like these test my vulnerability and challenge my parenting skills to the core. Time and again I've had to say to those around me, with tears streaming down my face, "I do not need security I can handle this."

Children with autism often have no filters or social rule etiquette that indicates to them what society deems as acceptable. My youngest child is so severely affected, that all five senses can shift into "meltdown" mode at the blink of an eye. My own senses have become adept at recognizing his energy shift and I defensively prepare for action. The sudden screaming in the middle a mall or huge public event surrounded by hundreds of people, jolts me into flight or fight mode and my nervous system reacts. I unconsciously prepare to tackle the situation, having no time to think about being vulnerable, it just happens. I am fully exposed whether I like it or not. The stares I get from strangers, their faces showing shock, disbelief, and rudeness crash into me with condemnation, leaving me feeling vulnerable and scared. In these moments I am unconsciously standing in my vulnerability and allowing myself to be courageously authentic. As a parent of children with autism, there is no way of choosing to not be vulnerable and hide. During these intense public meltdowns the inner child in me often becomes terrified. I begin trembling from head to toe, just praying to God we can get out of this situation and back to the car before it gets worse. On the outside I wear my armor and shield, pretending to have things under control, inside I'm shaken to the core and feel as if I'm drowning with fear.

These are the days I hate the autism. I allow myself to feel the hatred; I am only human and these are my true feelings. That doesn't make me a bad person. I still love myself and the job I am doing as a parent. My daily challenges often feel insurmountable and rightfully so. Raising a child with autism, so fragile and prone to meltdowns, is a roller coaster ride that ranges from exhausting, to lonely, to exhilarating. I like to think that perhaps the universe chose me as a very special parent to teach the world about parenting children like these. Also, to teach me about being vulnerable, authentic, and learning to love myself throughout this difficult journey.

At times I am uncertain when this journey began,

because it's all such a blur. I guess my story begins many years ago when my boys were young and both were diagnosed with autism pretty close together. They are four years apart to the week. Autism and finding natural ways to manage it became my mission. My oldest was diagnosed with "Asperger syndrome" (AS) and my youngest with full blown "Autism." I honestly don't particularly like the word autism, not because I'm not accepting of their conditions, but because I feel the label treats them as deficient, having a disease, being separate, and negative. This causes us to become distracted and forget who they really are as individuals. The word appears to subdivide our kids, while screaming to the rest of the world that they are broken, not normal, and we need to fix them so they act like all the other "neuro-typical" children.

When most people hear my story of being the single parent of two children with autism, their immediate response is one of sorrow and grief and they often apologize. I have to tell them its fine. I am good, the boys are good, we are extremely happy and have come a long way. I don't like feeling like a victim. I have unique challenges that for whatever reasons have been given to me in this lifetime. I also have many blessings. Ironically autism is the reason I've kept on going after falling down a thousand times. I get back up and try again. It's kind of like the yin and the yang. It can be a curse and a blessing. At times I felt the autism robbed me of my life dreams and goals, but in reality it created many new journeys in unchartered territories.

The boy's diagnosis early on was shocking and I became numb. Then I felt like I was in the middle of a tornado. It's hard to recollect many of the details surrounding them as babies. Don't ask me when they first crawled, walked, talked, or slept through the night. I honestly don't remember. My memories are weak and unsure, not because I am a bad parent and was extremely disorganized in keeping those "baby books filled with special moments, but because I was overwhelmed and continue to feel so. My life has never felt normal. I've learned to breathe through it all.

The boy's father and I were not on the same page with their autism. We divorced when the boys were very young. Autism has so many challenges and it easily divides and rips families apart. There is a lot of stress. When one parent chooses to face the autism with denial, it makes life pretty tough. Denying the autism and not embracing it was something I could not deal with or understand. I chose to fiercely forge ahead alone. Onward I went, learning to take one step at a time.

My oldest has high functioning autism, struggling with the inherit traits of anxiety and uncertainty with change. Roughly seven when he was officially diagnosed, he was excessively verbal, never stopped asking questions, or obsessing about his latest subject. He climbed everything, was extremely hyper, hard to get to sleep, and could bolt away from me in a heartbeat. His obsessions over the years have been quite entertaining: letters, numbers, food, movies, and one summer it was jump rope while counting. I twirled a jump rope endlessly that summer. I had to learn see the humor, laugh and enjoy it.

My youngest has been a greater challenge and mystery at times. He was miserable as a baby, constantly crying, appearing distressed, and an extremely troubled sleeper. He also had his share of frequent health challenges including gastrointestinal problems and intermittent vomiting. He just couldn't tolerate much of anything in his stomach. He also had an aversion to food. When I say aversion, I mean full on aversion. He didn't want to eat food, any food. He currently persists with this dislike.

As a toddler he became very ill. Rashes upon rashes appeared all over his body and he was severely inflamed inside and out. I ran all over town from physician to physician looking for answers. The rashes were so severe I feared I was going to lose him. At this my faith in a higher source truly kicked in. I was blessed to connect with a gastroenterologist who diagnosed him. He basically was malnourished, not absorbing any nutrients, and allergic to proteins. I was told to put the autism on the back burner so we could focus on the nutritional deficiencies. The doctor recommended a very expensive formula that was going to help him recover. The formula immediately shifted my son and he started to thrive. His rashes began to subside and it was a blessing to have found relief and the assurance of having a Doctor who understood what was going on. I noticed he became a bit happier, more content, and his sleep improved slightly. My son stayed on this formula for several more years. It helped him grow physically, but I still felt like there were missing links. He still had numerous challenges, predominantly the behaviors that go along with autism.

A few years later I began to learn about alternative forms of medicine. I was introduced to a chiropractor who practiced kinesiology. I also started taking the boys to a physician who specialized in chelation therapy. We discovered they were both loaded with toxins and heavy metals. I felt a sense of hope. I started chelating the boys amazed at how many heavy metals we were dumping out of them. We also started numerous nutritional supplements and began looking closer at nutritional deficiencies. I harbored much anger surrounding the autism and the reasons for the toxins and heavy metals. Was it the childhood vaccines, food and water supply, environmental, or just the perfect storm of genetics along with all the toxins? I realized that there was not enough energy in me, nor enough time, to simmer over the whys. I had to keep focused on what was in front of me at the moment and continue forging onward.

From here I was introduced to a local herbalist who also worked with kinesiology. We continued using herbs, supplements, and various homeopathic remedies. The herbalist suggested I take my youngest off his formula and put him on an organic raw milk diet. He had muscle tested fine for it and I was open, determined to attempt any possible avenue that might remotely assist in reversing the autism ever so slightly. The raw milk diet shifted him to remarkable new avenues and I sensed neurologically things were transpiring. Within a few weeks, the potty training that we had been struggling for years suddenly just happened. Then, his mood improved and he looked healthier. I now had a refrigerator full of raw milk.

My faith and determination in helping my boys remained compelling. I just kept praying and trusting that I was on the right path. I had gone through so many fearful and traumatic events with my life, the boys, and the autism, that I somehow learned to trust the next step in front of me, even though I didn't know where that step was taking me.

As I continued my journey, I also continued my exploration of (CAM) complementary and alternative medicine practices, with the boys. I made a firm choice early on that I would stay clear of any pharmaceutical drugs and utilize holistic practices to manage the symptoms and behaviors. Alternative forms of medicine resonated with me and I was constantly engaged in the researching of mind body medicine practices that could assist. I was interested in benefiting from what western medicine and integrative medicine had to offer. This led me to apply to Saybrook University's Mind Body Medicine Program and I was accepted. I loved connecting with others who understood that kinesiology, biofeedback, energy medicine, hypnosis, chiropractic, nutrition, prayer, and diet all could play a significant role in the body. I continued to search for the missing links and for solutions to help improve the many symptoms of the autism.

I was feeling ambiguous with the steered direction society had put in place for my kids. All the "systems" were confusing, overwhelming, and didn't necessarily make sense. The IEP's (Individual Educational Plans) through the schools, the state paperwork, workers, schedules, meetings, and appointment's to recheck and make sure the autism was still there so the state funding could be kept in place, were inconceivable. Somehow, the magic fairy hadn't snuck into my home and disengaged the autism shut off button just quite yet.

In 2010 I made a huge decision to leave Michigan and move to Hawaii. I had no family or friends there, but I wasn't concerned. Many around me thought I was crazy. I heard the whispers and imagined stories that ranged anywhere from, I was running from life to, I just couldn't handle the disappointments of having children with autism and how they didn't reach illustrious accomplishments like their peers. I was thankful for those who understood and realized it was my spiritual pursuit and not because I was checking out of life or hiding from the world. In fact it was just the opposite.

I went to Hawaii because the voice in me, that inner voice, kept saying "why not move to Hawaii?" My inner knowing said it was time and I trusted that voice. I had reached my limit with the deathly cold winters in Michigan and the winters were not harmonious with my children's health either. Was I making a big mistake listening to my inner guidance? I didn't think so. How would I know if I didn't try? Even if I fell flat on my face, at least I could say I tried. God knows I have made wrong choices in my life, we all have. I firmly believe that taking the wrong path at times, escorts us to surprising new beginnings.

I spent about four years living in and exploring Hawaii. I loved every part of my experience. I am extremely proud of myself for taking the plunge and being brave enough to challenge myself with such an immense move. It felt extremely empowering. One thing I learned through this process was being authentic and brave enough to live my life based on what I believe is right and not allowing other people's opinion's to hinder my decisions. If I had listened to those around me I would not have gone to Hawaii.

I've learned to embrace my truth and am fearless enough to share it with the world. For many years I lost my identity, forgetting who I was. I got caught in the cycle of parenthood and becoming hyper focused on my kids; they are a ton of work and have countless needs. I'm urging all you parents of children with autism to stop for a moment and breathe. Everything is going to be okay. I know most days are unpredictable and we ride the roller coaster of emotions with our kids. Many days I don't know whether to laugh, cry, or scream out loud with frustration. Some days I choose to do all three. We must be willing to surrender to all the unknowns. Breathe, relax, and let go.

Just recently I left Hawaii and moved back to the mainland. I miss it terribly. There were so many pros and cons of living there. It was a surreal experience and I have no regrets, but I ultimately became frustrated with the lack of support and services. Nonetheless, Hawaii is a wonderful environment to raise children with autism. The weather is perfect year round. Daily walks to the ocean, spotting dolphins and whales, and evening sunsets created an immense amount of meditative and calming experiences. The air is cleaner and the lifestyle casual. People are friendlier and resonate more from the heart. The slowed down lifestyle seemed to resonate well with my son's autism. What I most loved about Hawaii, was observing my youngest being so happy while sitting in nature, away from others and silently just being, practicing his own form of mindfulness. His nonverbal behaviors became less important and I was amazed.

For now, I sit here feeling extremely vulnerable wondering why I am back on the mainland. There is no plan. I will continue my path of living mindfully and authentically. I will continue my daily self-care with my mind and body and my loving relationship with myself. I will continue to speak my truth and trust my inner compass that I am back here for a reason. I know that time will reveal the "why." I am attempting to surrender to God's plan to find some comfort and peace in this time of transition. I continue to be grateful for all the gifts in my life and will continue to expect miracles for me, my boys, and all the other families who are on their own journeys through the maze of autism.

Kathleen Stroman has extensive experience in the field of mind body medicine which has been the cornerstone of her life for many years. Kathleen has found efficacy in combining a wide variety of alternative, holistic, and nutritional treatment options with her boys diagnosed with autism.

She holds a Master's of Science degree in Mind Body Medicine (MBM) and is currently earning a PhD in MBM with Saybrook University. She is a massage therapist, health and wellness coach, culinary and nutrition educator, and energy and informational medicine practitioner with Inergetix-CoRe who specializes in working with individuals with autism and their families.
kathleenastroman@gmail.com
www.kathleenstroman.com

Natasha Edwina

12 WHEN THE UNIVERSE CALLS

I sat on my bedroom floor, immobilized by stress. I was surrounded by piles of credit card and student loan statements and trying to figure out what went so terribly wrong. I owed more than my yearly income and was no longer able to make even the minimum payments. It was the year 2000, the turn of the millennium. At age twenty-three I was experiencing a turning point in my own personal evolution and my own Y2K meltdown.

Just before I re-carpeted my bedroom with credit card statements, I had awoken from a twenty-three hour slumber. This was a pivotal event that finally activated my self-concern. I am a heavy weight sleeper, but this was an all-time record. Something was very wrong. Ignoring the twenty extra pounds I had gained and the fact that I was punishing myself with junk foods, was a subtle type of self-harm. I was also, in both a literal and a metaphorical sense, biting off too much in my life. I was run down and not noticing the dark circles under my eyes, as I tried to suppress the loneliness and the loss of hope for a better future. I had a college degree, yet couldn't financially support myself and the debt kept getting bigger and bigger. Stress dreams and nightmares were common. I was frequently ill and had developed allergies. Having health insurance was one of the few things I was grateful for.

Several things led up to this dark place. In my last year of college, my mother and stepfather had a messy divorce and my mother remarried and moved out of state. The divorce from my biological father had been very conflictual as well and I was sad to see my younger half-siblings go through it too. However, with this event I was finally completely free from any ties to my oldest stepbrother, who had sexually molested me from the time I was a toddler. My younger half-brother had just left for Germany with the army. My family that had been together for about twenty years suddenly dispersed.

After graduation I moved cross-country from Wisconsin to Arizona; I had decided I was done with snow. Having only $300 and a job interview with a non-profit social services agency, I luckily landed on my feet and got the job, but the starting pay was only $22,500/year. That was less than I made waiting tables while a student. I loved how important my work was, but it was emotionaly demanding. As a survivor, I had much empathy and compassion to offer the children I was working with. However, having my own trauma, I was additionally regularly exposed to secondary trauma at work and my sensitivity made it hard to not take the job home with me. My heart broke for those kids.

I was in a vulnerable place and further stressed with acclimating to a new regional culture and living independently. During a visit to Arizona, my then sixteen year old half-sister disclosed to me that she was also molested by our oldest brother. I reported him and the whole ordeal was devastating. I had done everything to protect her, even going to the point of taking her out of that home. Yet, what I feared most happened to her. I couldn't save myself, but I had so wanted to save her and couldn't. At the same time I was validated in knowing that I had not imagined what happened to me. All those old negative feelings I had buried for so long surfaced. Adding them to everything else I was experiencing crushed me. There was too much for me to cope with, sending me into a depressive tailspin and the twenty-three hours of sleep I began this story with.

Why was able to take action for her when I couldn't for myself? I needed to know the answer to that question. I began an important healing journey, but I had to go through a dark night of the soul.

I had some major health issues for someone of my age and ended up on two overlapping rounds of antibiotics, which seems to have changed my digestive system permanently. Experiencing severe gastrointestinal issues caused me to fear I had Crohn's disease. I was referred to a specialist who prescribed more medications.

One of my earliest coping skills was numbing everything out and I had gotten so good at it. But, it almost killed me when I needed my body to alert me of danger. At the age of fourteen, I walked around for two weeks with appendicitis not recognizing how ill I was. Eventually the pain became severe and I dreamt that I was falling into a black hole, while my family waved goodbye to me as I reached for their hands. I woke up sobbing and scared and went to the hospital the next day. I almost died in surgery because of the amount of poison in my abdomen from an appendix that had ruptured the previous week. Coming out of surgery to hear this was quite a powerful spiritual awakening for me. I realized that since I was spared there must be some reason for me to still be here.

Yet, almost ten years later, I seemed to have forgotten, slipping into such a numbed out existence by eating too much, drinking too much, and spending too much. I also loved too much; everyone but myself. After that twenty-three hour sleep session, I knew I had to see a doctor. My blood work came back normal, so I was referred to a warm and lovely psychiatrist, just the type you would want to see in a situation like this. He did not treat my illness like a chronic disease. He asked if I'd like to "try" an antidepressant, as if it would be something to just get me through this period in my life. He told me there was a fairly new type of antidepressant called Wellbutrin, which helped with sleepy fatigued types of depression, without causing sexual side effects or weight gain.

My body seemed just as resistant to medication as my mind was and I had to work up to a near maximum dosage before my body finally succumbed. The first thing I noticed when it began to take effect was that I was now sleeping eight hours and awakening refreshed. Colors seemed more vibrant and I now had a sense of hope that I could do something about my situation. Feeling better, I realized how bad the depression was and how guilty and worthless I had felt. Also, how badly I was treating myself out of self-loathing. I was not seeing a therapist yet, (I initially had treatment as a child after disclosing the abuse) but at work I had access to some great workbooks on healing from sexual abuse. I had moved out of "freeze" and was now in "fight or flight," finally in action.

Taking action, I put my credit cards into debt consolidation, quit my second job as a cocktail waitress, and spent my free time reading and doing workbook pages. The medication was a real blessing, but I knew it wasn't a long-term solution. I decided to train for a marathon and had muscle testing for food allergies; testing positive for gluten, dairy, and corn. This led to me reading everything I could about nutrition. I read the book *Eat Right for Your Blood Type* which helped me see the dangers of consuming processed foods, dairy, and grains. Changing my diet significantly improved my intestinal issues.

I really loved the book *Body for Life* which helped me get into the best shape ever by introducing me to the concept of six small meals per day, balanced blood sugar, interval training, and proper resistance training. The author even built in goal setting into his book along with the concept of a free day. The twelve week program took me two years to complete successfully, but when I did, it was a habit for life. I joined a women only gym for $4/month, where I felt comfortable working out without it being a scene. I talked to a nutritionist there who recommended natural supplements that would help my mood, such as omega-3's and conjugated linoleic acid (CLA), along with physical fitness. I had previously been taking Hydroxycut (it contained ephedra back then) and in retrospect I think a large piece of my depression was adrenal exhaustion from the stimulants, coffee, two jobs, PTSD, and ongoing stress of pushing myself too hard. I also started treating myself to massage and it was a healing experience to have healthy touch and nurture my body at the same time.

At the women's gym, I joined my first yoga class. The teacher was very gifted at guided meditation and would do a beautiful Shavasana at the end, consisting of breathing through mists of the colors of the chakras and connecting us with the wisdom and the support of the Universe. Those weekly classes resulted in major shifts in my stress levels, my eating habits, and my acceptance and appreciation of my body. I began to care for myself, learned to listen to my body's wisdom, and treated myself in more loving and gentle ways.

At this time quite out of the blue, I fell in love. The first time I saw him, the rest of the room just faded away. We met up later that week and were pretty much inseparable after that, connecting on a very deep level. What unfolded for us was a beautiful relationship that gave me faith in life and love again. It was a safe and secure place to explore myself deeper and grow, inspiring me to be my best. I began to see a mind-body therapist to work on my next level of emotional healing and be the best partner I could be.

I did a lot of work between sessions. Using tuition reimbursement from my employer, I attended local health seminars where I learned about mind-body health, energy healing, feng shui, and color therapy. I also became acquainted with the work of Louise Hay and came across three books that year that changed my life and my career path forever: *Awakening Intuition* by Dr. Mona Lisa Shulz, *Body Mind* by Ken Dychtwald, and *Women's Bodies Women's Wisdom* by Dr. Christiane Northrup. All of these books took me into the fascinating study of how emotions are held in the body and impact physical health. I learned health conditions could be resolved by addressing the underlying emotions and that we could be the source of our own healing, by tapping into our intuition. As I devoured these three books I was inspired to not only apply the knowledge to myself, but to make mind-body health a career path.

By this time I was very fit, almost forty pounds lighter than I was during my depression hibernation. More importantly, I had energy to spare, mental clarity, and peace. My inner light was shining brightly again like it was always meant to, but hadn't since I was two or three years old. I had my finances under control and became so good at budgeting that I was able to move into my own little studio apartment.

Inspired by the books I had been reading and my growing restlessness with my job, I decided that I wanted to work with individuals on a deeper level. I was being called to return to school for credentials to help guide others through the transformation I had gone through. I knew quitting my job and returning to school meant I would lose my health insurance and would no longer be able to afford antidepressant medication. Feeling so good with my own self-designed integrative healthcare plan, I felt that these lifestyle changes would be my medicine. I requested that my psychiatrist taper me off of the medication and I replaced it with amino acids, optimal nutrition to avoid depression, and continued exercise.

The graduate program I wanted did not exist yet, (I had been searching for years) so I found a well-respected and fully accredited university with an integrative psychology program. I was thrilled to see that it was in a city that I loved, a city that felt oddly familiar to me the first time I visited, San Diego. They accepted me into a one year intensive masters in Psychophysiology and Biofeedback. Through a twist of fate I instead began a masters in Marriage and Family Therapy. I wanted to understand the scientific connection between mind and body in order to help others achieve optimal health in a holistic way, as well as be accepted by mainstream healthcare professionals and institutions. When the Biofeedback program was cancelled, the admissions coordinator convinced me that MFT (a study of systems and relationships) was by nature a holistic theory of health. I was told I could have my own private practice and integrate holistic methods. What they didn't tell me is that it might take ten years to finish the program and be fully licensed - it's good that they didn't, or I wouldn't have done it.

In order to save for the move to San Diego for graduate school, I took a second job as a cocktail waitress. My boyfriend and I broke up just before I moved; he was also feeling called to pursue his soul desires independently. The break-up was like a piece of my soul ripping away. Luckily, I was otherwise the healthiest I had ever been and sublimated the pain into excitement for a new life chapter.

My education and training in MFT, although extremely rigorous and labor intensive, became a deeply healing experience that I didn't know I needed. The Universe tends to work in this way. I added as many classes as I could from the Integrative Psychology program as electives and my mind was blown open. This was the beginning of another spiritual awakening. By this time, I was enjoying school so much that I decided to stay on for the doctoral degree, post masters. However, I ran out of financial aid and out of steam.

My days were incredibly busy and hectic between school, job, and practicum (where I worked for free). The stress caught up with me and I was crying frequently. I finally quit my bartending job to relieve some pressure and had some trouble finding a job in my field. I was now in a dark area again. My car broke down, I had to move, and I was unemployed for three months and living off of credit cards. Eventually I was back in a job only slightly different from the one I left in Phoenix and took a second restaurant job to supplement my income. As I collected 3000 client therapy hours toward licensure, I was extremely impatient to be doing what I set out to do.

Spending a lot of time contemplating the direction my life was going, I realized by now that I wanted to be a mother within the next five years. My intention then was to prepare myself mind, body, and soul. Realizing I still had more healing to do, I focused again on nutrition, exercise, and overcoming past trauma that was still evident in some occasional nightmares. I also went back into therapy. Soon afterwards, a friend I had a romantic history with, started working at the restaurant as well; sparks flew again and I fell in love.

The Universe had not forgotten the plan, because a baby came much quicker than either of us intended. What an amazing physical and emotional experience pregnancy was! It was everything I had hoped for and more. I was very good at nurturing myself so that I could nurture my baby. She was my whole focus. I soon became aware that the standard of care I had for my baby was higher than I had for myself. After this awareness I began treating myself as if I was just as precious as I was when I was carrying the baby, even after I was done breastfeeding.

My pregnancy with my son took self-love and self-care further and it was an intensely meaningful experience for me, as I was being trained by the Center for Mind-Body Medicine while pregnant with him. I connected with my baby boy in utero through meditation, guided imagery, nutrition, movement and spirituality. Practicing these modalities helped me keep stress manageable during the pregnancy. My son is one of the most laid back, sweet, and funny little guys you will ever meet. I was able to birth him naturally in my home with a midwife, because I now trusted my body and knew what it was capable of.

The healthy habits I adopted during both my pregnancies have remained with me and have shaped our family's healthy lifestyle. Compulsive eating and punishing myself with food naturally disappeared and never returned. I couldn't possibly ever be ashamed of my body again after experiencing its creative power and sheer strength during the pregnancies and childbirth process. I absolutely adored breastfeeding my children. I experienced so much appreciation and love for my breasts that fed and nurtured my children so profoundly. It was such a healing ritual for my body that had been misused so many years ago.

Though my journey of learning to love myself will always be a work in progress, I am in a very good place. I have an amazing family. I am supported by healthy, loving, inspiring, like-minded colleagues and friends. I AM healthy, loving, and inspirational! I am doing exactly what I set out to do by earning a PhD in Mind-Body Medicine, specializing in Integrative Mental Health, and joining the ranks of others leading a paradigm shift in mainstream healthcare.

This year I had the opportunity to meet and thank my heroes Dr. Mona Lisa Shulz and Dr. Christiane Northrup, whose books and courageous wisdom were a beacon of light in this inspired journey and career path for me. As a coach and a therapist I am honored and humbled to work with clients each day who inspire me with the light within them and their limitless creative possibilities. I dream of inspiring others and creating a positive ripple of love, health, happiness, compassion and peace throughout the world.

Natasha Edwina is a Certified Mindful Coach, Licensed Marriage and Family Therapist, speaker, author, and mother of two. She is completing a PhD in Mind-Body Medicine specializing in Integrative Mental Health. Her passion is to inspire individuals to live more peaceful, loving, empowered, and healthy lives.

Her main interests are optimal nutrition, mental health, spirituality, transformation, transcending oppression.

Natasha operates a private integrative psychotherapy practice in San Diego and an international coaching and consulting business, Oasis of Awareness. She facilitates mind-body skills groups integrating research-based mind-body techniques, nutrition, and group support for a whole mind-body-spirit transformative experience. More information at: www.oasisofawareness.com.

Deeanna Burleson

13 A WINDING PATH TO LOVE

Loving myself is a phrase that at one point in my life I could have never even have thought about, much less discussed. After all, I grew up like many, being told all that was wrong with me: how I looked, how I acted, how I dressed, what I thought, what I did not think, what I wrote, how I wrote. These negative statements even occurred as I announced my intention to write this account of my experiences with authenticity and loving myself, "I never thought you had it in you."

In the world and culture I was born, grew from a baby to a "mature" adult, I learned to behave and often act (a very appropriate word) as I was expected to, whether that was at the core of my being or not. The path to being authentic for me first began with discovering and then accepting who I am (who I was). Then loving all parts of me that others and I had been critical of in the past. These criticisms still creep into my thoughts, but I can for the most part let them go. This journey has been long and continues to this day. For me this is a primary purpose of life, to learn to love and respect myself so that I can truly love others. When we become self-aware we see our shadows (the things we have been hiding). These emotions and beliefs are colliding within us and by our refusal to give them voice, we suppress our authentic self, becoming silent.

When the light of awareness bumps up against concrete form, a shadow is cast.

So, too, does knowledge imitate observation. They can resemble each other, but never completely.

A blind person filled with awe-inspiring wonder has more vision than anyone full of knowledge.

Awareness, observation and a smile alone are real. All else fades like clouds in the morning sun.

Authenticity, by Ajna Wata

Ah, awareness, that is where it all began for me. Awareness of things and of behaviors accepted in my culture, but that did not feel right, did not feel like it aligned with who I was and who I wanted to be. If we just accept and live as we are told based on others expectations and cultural lenses, then we are not aware, but are just living as robots. The awareness of those internal nudges, the things, the work, is what excites. Cheryl Peppers and Allen Briskin describe in their book, *Bringing your Soul to Work*, the impact of a discrepancy between the life we lead and the worlds that collide in our heart. The impact is a feeling of being empty and superficial. I often tried to behave as I was expected to, only find a huge collision of emotions, outcomes, and not what I had planned. Oh, if I only had a crystal ball that worked, I could plan my life better! Yes, I am still shaking my head in amazement of the journey and experiences that would become my lessons in authenticity, loving myself, and finding the real purpose for my life.

THE BEGINNINGS

I was born in the 1950's to two loving parents and into a southern, rural area. At that time, civil and women rights were hot topics and a new way of being was emerging. My parents both were employed in textiles. My father finished the 6th grade and my mother had attended two years of business school prior to marrying my father. From a very early age I questioned the way people of color were treated, even though my community and the nation were steeped in prejudice. The Ku Klux Klan had members in my community and for a time, a training location a few miles from my house. When I was around six years of age, I asked a dear Uncle and Aunt (like parents) who had brought great stability to my young life, to take me to the black section of town to find a "black" mamma. They laughed and told my mom who also found it funny. To this day I have no idea what prompted me to ask this and do not understand why I was not as prejudiced as everyone around me. I have never been concerned with the color or race of a person. I do observe behavior and look for the causes of the behavior.

Throughout my childhood my mother would say frequently, "I wish I had done..." there were many endings to this sentence. My mind converted her desires into, "I will never say or desire to have done something that I did not at least try." This thought has made me very determined and often quick to act on things "I think" I want to do or should do. I believe this thought embedded deep into my subconscious, has been responsible for where I am today and the experiences along the way. It has been the foundation and possibly even the energy to my awareness, authenticity and learning to love myself.

Even though my parents were very loving to me, there was much conflict in the home. My parents were wonderful and did the best they could with what they were dealing within themselves. I have to add at this point, that we all come into this life with our challenges and our shadow self that is often hidden. This conflict propelled my determined self to marry at a very young sixteen years of age. "My plan" was that I would create "my perfect family." Not long after I left home to marry, my brother was born. Although we never lived together in the same house, I have always felt a strong connection to him and love him dearly. Of course, this plan of creating "my perfect family" did not play out as I had imagined. After many years of searching for that *Ozzie and Harriet* family, I realized what I was searching for did not exist. I have realized through my life that any relationship whether marriage, children, brother, other important family, or dear friends, was not based on my proving something or my creating and making those happen. It was based on honoring and respecting others where they were, with their challenging life lessons and hard relationship work.

The most valuable thing I lost or marginalized along the way to my pursuit of doing and being, was real connection with my childhood friends and many family members, including my wonderful brother as well as precious time with my two daughters, truly my heart. I was too focused on proving to myself and others that I was worthy, that I was smart, that I was somebody important in this world, in a culture that valued money and status symbols. Now as I look back, what I believed was needed then to achieve a stable life feels so foreign to my current beliefs and awareness. I saw a happy "appearing" family that consisted of husband, wife and children, a Mercedes as a car, a Tudor style house, and nice clothes bought from high-end stores. Those represented a stable life to me, the perfect life I was trying to create. I now know that stability is being self-aware, authentic, and discovering who I am in addition to the passions I bring to this earth.

This awareness as you can imagine did not occur overnight. It took me many years of being knocked down, placed mentally and often physically in gut wrenching, depressed fetal like positions; times when I was afraid to go to sleep because it might be worse the next day. It was only after creating situations that hurt people, not intentionally but subconsciously, so that I could prove my worth, that I discovered what was really important in life for me and that was, relationships and people.

An experience in my teenage years should be shared because it was a very defining moment and motivated me toward my academic and professional pursuits. This was my experience with religion and my Christian beliefs. I encountered "leaders" of the Christian faith who did not exhibit love and respect for human beings. My question was always how those religious leaders could say they were Christian, when they did not exhibit any behaviors that demonstrated love for others. After all, was that not the first commandment of Christ, who they worshipped and represented? My internal compass told me something was wrong and I ran from organized religion, but continued to feel the presence of a spiritual being with me very frequently throughout the years.

I still continue to possess a very strong faith and spirituality, but not in the context of domineering and controlling environments. I have a strong belief in a divine being, but not in human beings, not in male or female religious leaders. After all, they are human with the same struggles as you and I. Over the years and through experiences I found places of worship where I could grow in my spirituality and love for the divine, as well as my fellow human beings.

Now, I try to do all I can to respect and embrace others in my interactions and conversations. Do I perfectly achieve this 100% of the time? No, but I am striving. The awareness of how I felt and why I acted the way I did, allowed me to be aware of the emotions those actions resulted from. This also led me to seeing people in the same light as I saw myself, individuals battling emotions that are embedded deep within their unconscious, with behaviors and actions that are rooted in fear and survival, just like me.

ACADEMICS, CAREER AND PROFESSIONAL

At a very early age of five, I decided I wanted to be a nurse, after the experience of several eye surgeries beginning at age one. I remember someone asked me one day, "what if you can't be a nurse?" I quickly and emphatically said, "I guess I will have to be a doctor."

After I married, finished high school and delivered my first beautiful daughter, I attended a local community college for a one-year licensed practical nurse program where I graduated with honors. I loved patient care and I loved health care. After a few years I applied to a university and attended a four-year bachelor program in nursing. By this time I was a single mother, raising two beautiful daughters. Through the help of a dear friend and my mother, I was able to balance all the requirements of work, school, and parenting, at least in my mind. I believed and told myself I was doing all of this to create that perfect life for my children. The reality was, that perfect life had been left behind in the pursuit of proving myself and not missing out on any opportunity.

Once I had received my bachelors in nursing, I joined the Air National Guard as a flight nurse. Yes, another requirement, but remember, I felt I could do it all and create that perfect life. This commitment came with military requirements, in addition to civilian work requirements, which resulted in my working almost every weekend in any given month. My military career lasted for twenty-six years. I retired as a Lieutenant Colonel from an active duty assignment working for the U.S. Joint Chief of Staff for the Surgeon who advised the Chairman of the Joint Staff. The opportunities and travel I experienced over those years were amazing. I can say, without a shadow of doubt, that everywhere I traveled around the world I thought, "I wish my daughters were here so we could experience these adventures together." How insane this seems now, as I look back over the last almost forty years

In addition to the exciting experiences in the military, I had very interesting opportunities in the civilian and Veterans Administration sectors of health care. They ranged from nursing in emergency departments, to nursing in intensive care units. Also, hospital supervisor, administration for emergency department, computerized documentation systems, and home care. Then, bringing it all together as a risk manager for a large health care system, I accepted a position at a large international consultant firm in Washington, D.C. to conduct program evaluation visits. Now I was able to bring everything I had ever done and wanted to do in a powerful way . I would be changing organizations by increasing the awareness of those involved and unleashing their potential.

So many experiences and I would never have to say I wish I had done something, because I was doing it all. All except creating that stable appearance and reality of family life that I thought was driving this constant activity, this striving to prove myself for so many years.

There have been many defining experiences in my career where I was able have a glimpse of my authentic self. Once I was in a mentorship training class in the VA Healthcare System and I was asked to tell the group something they may not know about me. My first, quick response without thinking was that I really love people. I surprised myself with that response but it felt real, it felt authentic. I remember to this day feeling no fear that people in the group would think I was being insincere, mushy, or weird. It was just the way it was. Over the years there have been other defining moments that provided me with a look into who I was at the time. I shifted from wishing I had a crystal ball, to just listening for internal guidance and then, to being thankful for those *breadcrumbs of life* as I call them. These *breadcrumbs of life* continue to assure me I am on the right path and going through the right doors. They assure me I am engaging in the correct type of interaction with all those wonderful human beings that cross my path while walking theirs.

TODAY, AS IT IS AT THIS MOMENT

Several years ago after I retired from the military. When I was working for that large international consulting firm, making more money than I had ever made in my life, I was able to have those symbols of stability; not a Mercedes but a BMW, clothes from high end stores, vacations for my family and myself. However, I remained single, living on a sailboat in Washington, DC. My daughters had not only survived a non-traditional mother, but had become wonderful, beautiful, caring human beings and we were very close and connected.

There came a point where I was so compromised with my belief system and the expectations for me in the work environment, that a huge state of internal collision occurred. I quit my position, thinking I would rather be homeless than compromise my being. I returned to the southern state of my youth to care for my mother and to an academic setting in the pursuit a PhD program. For several years I had been pulled to find a doctoral program to work in Global Health. Then, I felt the nudge to find a program where I could build my skills to hopefully improve the healthcare environment. Over the years I have observed first-hand how non-caring many healthcare environments are, to family members, patients, staff or leaders. The effects of being in these environments included stress, disease, conflict, and just a poor state of being. I had experienced positive outcomes from non-traditional therapies such as massage, yoga, music, contemplation, and reading which allowed me to survive some brutal emotional and physical insults to my being. I believed that if I could help create caring environments in our healthcare organizations, our families and communities would achieve a higher level of well-being, strength, and capability.

This PhD experience in Organizations Systems has

not been about securing a big job or proving myself once again; it's about continuing my exploration of my authentic self and giving that self a language and avenue for courageous expression, in a loving and caring manner. I have discovered for myself that the real secret to being awake and fully living life is in relationship with others. Meaning and strength in our lives is created, with respect and acceptance, in our relationships with our families, our communities, and organizations. It is created in relationship with the person we meet on the street, in the store, the unexpected person, the driver on the road. It is about how we embrace their humanness through being aware of our own state of being human

The focus of my research and studies is on integrative health systems, the concept of well-being and patient centered care. In addition to my PhD studies and research, I offer to individuals and organizations avenues and tools for finding their strength within, because at the foundation of an organization or an individual there is the human component that is powerful beyond measure, but who often needs permission and the ability to tap into that amazing, complex system the Divine has created.

Today I have as many interactions with my family and friends as possible. I am married to a wonderful man, not in a *Harriet and Ozzie* existence, but in mutual respect, working hard together for our life. If the phone rings, I answer and put down whatever I am doing because odds are I am doing something. Because of my life experiences, positive and negative, and then the peeling back, removing the layers of deep rooted emotions through self-awareness, ensuring self-care and accepting who I am at this very moment, I am able to continue down the very windy path of learning to love and respect myself moment by moment.

So now, go to a mirror and look deep into your eyes and tell yourself that you are wonderful and that you love the person in that mirror. My hope is that you will ask yourself about your authenticity and that you will be courageous enough to go exploring. The only time that really counts, is this very moment in time. My wish for you is that you will have the courage to find your amazing strength on your winding earthly path.

Deeanna Burleson is owner of Full Spectrum Solutions, an organization system consultant, and a guide for individuals and organizations in finding their inner strength, power and higher levels of well-being. Her approaches contain respect for the other and where they are on this journey of life on earth. She motivates and guides others to learn to live a more content and inspired life. She is available for organizational development approaches, program evaluation and analysis, workshops and humanistic approaches, in groups and individual sessions to discover that inner strength and state of well-being.
Email: fullspectrumsolns@gmail.com
Cell: 703-303-6143

Cassandra Lyons

14 CONNECTING WITHIN TO LOVE

My journey of learning to love myself began long ago in a land far away, in another time and dimension. It was at this time that I decided to stop looking outside of myself for love and instead to learn and grow through the love hereinhat I Am. It was a time when I realized that I was here for this very expansion and that I was not only a part of God, or this beautiful Universe, I was an extension of it. But it was through this life that I was to truly remember this. Being an extension of God/Source Energy as a human, has allowed me to grow and expand through every experience in my life, the hard times as much as the joyful times. These experiences have shaped me into the woman I am today and I am forever grateful; for herein lies the story of how I learned to love myself, deeply.

I don't know that I ever really "felt" what it meant to love myself until I was inspired to create *Dancing 365 Days to Raise Vibration* in February of 2014. But this is something I will share more at the end of this chapter. I would first like to share some of my most powerful and defining moments.

As I look back on my childhood, one thing I have always felt, is a deep connection with God and the beautiful Universe that we live in. Some kids dream of being Doctors or Teachers, but my dream was to be an Astronaut and explore the unknown. Each day growing up was a new adventure full of wonder and treasures to be discovered. I could hardly wait to spend time outside playing and laughing with my neighborhood friends, or just spend time alone. In the summers I would play outside until the streetlights came on. That was the rule in our family, when the streetlights came on, that was the time to head home. This was the time in my life I felt free being me.

Amongst the freedom and joy filled times, I also experienced some pretty significant losses. When I was one and a half years old my birth father left. When I was five, my baby brother died at birth and I never had the change to know him. When I was nine, my adopted father left. With all this loss With all this loss I felt confused, sad, and like the bottom had fallen out from underneath me. I felt I had lost everything that I had known about security in my life. These "losses" began to reshape my foundation and understanding of what love was, as well as beginning to understand the love between a father and daughter. I also believed that love was something outside of me; something that was based on the conditions of what I did, or how I behaved. This led to a need for constant reassurance to make me feel that I was okay. Without this reassurance, I felt anxiety and worry about being abandoned. Thankfully, the love that I received from my Mother was consistent and beautiful, the kind of love that makes you feel invincible and alive. Never once did I doubt the love that I was receiving from my Mother, which was such an amazing experience to have as a young girl. Since shifting my feelings and beliefs, both my birth father and adopted father are present in my life today.

As I matured, I began to bring this new awareness of what I believed love was into relationships, whether intimate or friendships. Dancing between these lines of intimacy and friendship with boys and flirting with the edges of both at the same time, I felt confused. I felt new sensations in my whole being as my hormones were coming to life. I was also walking this edge of not really knowing what being loved by a boy really meant to me. At that time I was like many other teenagers, feeling and thinking about what I needed most, which was to feel connection and belonging with my peers. I discovered in Junior High that I had a strong need/desire to be liked by others. I often put my own needs aside for others, sometimes to the detriment of my wellbeing. I wasn't aware at the time that I had developed a very strong fear of losing people, so I did whatever it took to fit in and be liked. I am grateful to have a mother who instilled very good morals and beliefs that were also flowing within me and helping to guide me along, with a very strong connection to God and the Universe.

Dancing has also provided an amazing amount of guidance throughout my life and is something that I have loved to do ever since I was six. I studied ballet and jazz from Bonnie Haney in my hometown of Moorhead, Minnesota. Bonnie really helped me to connect to dance in a beautiful and meaningful way. She inspired me not just as a dancer, but also provided a strong platform for me to grow as a young child into a young woman. Since I had this strong platform I was free to explore my body and emotions in the class and on stage. These opportunities gave me the opening to connect even deeper within, so that I could move freely out into the world. It wasn't until I was much older that I realized what dancing did for me. When I did have this awareness it was an understanding that I am most connected to God/ Source Energy when I dance.

With dance being a big part of my life, it helped me to find my place and remain connected within, during complicated teenage years. It was something that I exceled at and felt good about. One male relationship that was very powerful and meaningful for me was with a friend, Fidel. He knew how to breakdance and I wanted to learn how. Many days after school we broke down a cardboard box, threw it on the floor and he then patiently taught me how to breakdance. It meant so much to me that if he was attracted to me, he never let that influence our interactions. In fact, he treated me with such kindness, that it allowed me to feel totally free to be myself. I didn't feel like I needed to be worried about what he thought, felt, or what he was thinking, because he treated me like a human being, an extension of God. I felt seen by him and respected.

At this time in my life I didn't yet know that I was a deliberate creator and that I co-create with God and All That Is. I didn't know that I was a being of light and love and that all of these experiences that I was having were helping me, shaping my understanding of who I am, and what love is to me. The unfolding of this beautiful experience is one that I hold close to me, a moment in time when I caught a glimpse of the love that is me. This one I cherish, as well as the other moments in time when I had lost sight of the love that is me. For it is also through the "hard" times that we grow and gain great clarity of what we truly want and desire. I now call these times the *Compost*. What is compost? It's something that stinks, and is gross. But what does it do? It makes things grow into beautiful plants or flowers. So the hard times are essential to our growth even if they are painful. I too had many painful moments, like a lot of people in this world. All of which I know now, were a part of a bigger plan.

When I was young, playing and hanging out with neighborhood guy friends was something I always did. As I matured into a young woman, there were small and large moments of awkwardness and pain; defining moments where the lines blurred between friendships and relationships. This made for a very confusing time for me, full of mixed emotions, while interacting with my guy friends. This often left me feeling unloved and with an even stronger desire to be loved. I desired love and attention from a male so much, that this became my focus; to "find" the young man that would make me feel the love that I was seeking.

As I moved through my teenage years into my 20's and late 30's, I felt that I was not complete unless I was dating someone. I somehow felt I was not good enough. This wasn't a conscious thought, but was more like a desperate need, a "space" to be filled. Most don't know how to fill that space, until they discover it through mountains of pain and suffering. How I went about filling this space became some of my greatest lessons of learning to love myself. For most of my life my attention was focused outward in my journey to fill this space. I began by trying to fill it with one relationship after another; thinking that one day there would be the "right" relationship and that space would be no more. The problem with trying to fill this emptiness in me was that trying to use a relationship to fill it never felt right. This meant that even when I was in the relationship the feeling of the "space" was still there, nagging at me. The men who I was attracting were also an issue, because they were men who either weren't that into me, or were emotionally or physically unavailable. This was the familiar pattern that I was used to. It wasn't what I truly desired, but it was what I was most comfortable with, someone leaving me.

I somehow never felt good enough. If I was in a relationship, it felt as though there was always something wrong with the relationship, the person, or me. There was always something I needed to fix within me or within them; so this became the focus instead of just enjoying it all. I never felt like I could fully relax, because I was always waiting for the other shoe to drop. I got into relationships where I was cheated on and lied to, continually reaffirming the belief that I was not good enough. I would give up what I was most interested in, or not communicate what was most important to me, for fear of this person leaving. Most of the time, I didn't even feel like I knew what I truly wanted, because I was trying to be what this other person wanted me to be. This was also true within my friendships. I was afraid that if I spoke my mind I would upset them and they would leave.

The major problem with trying to be something other than myself, was that I wasn't able to allow love in when it did come. I had many friends and boys who truly liked me, but I always questioned their admiration, thinking that they weren't being honest with me. This hindered my relationships and my ability to fully enjoy the life that I was living. What made this even more challenging, was that in high school people were drawn to me and whatever I put my mind to, I did really well. This was great, but I always ended up feeling really uncomfortable. I felt put in the spotlight which made me afraid to mess up. At the same time I also started to have some health issues with my digestion and fatigue. This made me feel that I wasn't able to fully show up in the way I wanted and was expected to, which created even more fears of being left and unloved.

The summer after I graduated from high school, just before entering college, I got Mono. I developed Chronic Fatigue and Candida Albicans and as a result was severely debilitated. Dancing was the main thing that helped me to cope with being sick. I felt the most well when I was dancing. I connected with people in a more joyful and playful way, at a time when I was most suffering and most disconnected from my wellbeing. When I wasn't dancing, I felt like an emotional and physical wreck. I was sitting in the *compost*, desiring to explore the world and yet my illness held me close to home, filled with fear and a growing anxiety. I felt like a bird, afraid to leave the nest and afraid that if I did, I wouldn't be able to fly.

I began college in the fall. My illness became a defining moment in my life for many reasons, one being that it created the focus of my studies and career path. Unfortunately I don't remember a whole lot of what I learned at that time, but what I did begin to learn was the life path that was calling me. I still spent a lot of time trying to fill that *space*, but I also spent a lot of time discovering what I liked and loved. I got to work in a planetarium teaching first year Astronomy students about the constellations. I also had another job with the school where I coordinated the Celebration of Nations, which allowed me the opportunity to meet people from many different countries. This was a huge passion of mine. I was a part of many of the Cultural Alliances where I got to learn even more about the different cultures and ethnicities around the World. But, even with all of these amazing experiences, I was still not fully living because of my illness and because I was still so focused on filling this empty *space* inside.

It wasn't until I graduated that I discovered I was capable of more. Graduating in itself was a huge accomplishment, because I had been so sick. The doors began to open, allowing me to explore life from a place of freedom, like when I was a child. This was the turning point for my stepping into my wellbeing. Right out of college I worked for an outdoor experiential education camp where I learned and taught kids how to sail, canoe, camp, and build campfires. I took a trip to Montana where I did my first real mountain biking. I hiked to the peak of mountains and explored trails alone. Then I moved to the boundary waters of Minnesota and worked at a canoe and outfitters lodge. I took a three day solo canoe trip and gained so much confidence in myself.

I decided to move to New Mexico and began to "find" and heal myself. This led me to enroll in Massage School and I became a Certified Massage Therapist which deepened my understanding of energy and healing, as well as a deeper healing within my own being. I gave birth to my beautiful baby girl, Livia, at home, which was one of the most amazing and best experiences of my life. I moved back to Minnesota and joined African drumming and dancing groups and then one of the most exciting things happened to me through my dancing, the opportunity to dance with Bobby McFerrin on Stage! This was a significant affirmation of the importance of dance in my life.

I became a single mom when my daughter was three and spent many years learning how to be happy and fully me, while being alone. I continued working as a massage therapist. Three year later, I became a certified Life Coach to transition into a new career. Then three years after that, I fell in love with my amazing boyfriend Jamie and I have been learning how to be me fully while being in this relationship. I made the commitment to work with a coach, Leslie who taught me so many amazing tools. One very important tool was how to take 100 percent responsibility for the experiences I have in my life. I joined Quantum Success Coaching Academy and became a Certified Law of Attraction Coach, which opened my eyes and changed my life. I am now living my life from a whole new paradigm.

Since living my life from this new paradigm I received the inspiration to create Dancing 365 Days to Raise Vibration. The intention for round one was, to raise my vibration. Each day I danced and uploaded a video to YouTube for an entire year. I finished the first year on February 11th, 2015! I began round two of Dancing 365 Days to Raise Vibration on February 14th, Valentine's Day. I set the intention for Round 2 to be about connecting within to the Love of who we are. This intention was to inspire myself, as well as those dancing with me to connect within and live from the place of love. I currently have 177 countries dancing/viewing to raise their vibrations with me every single day. The journey so far has been amazing! This is just the beginning of a beautiful new chapter in my life of connecting within, and allowing the love that is me to shine.

Dancing every day, plus the Law of Attraction and a lifetime of experiences not only has helped me to "feel" the love that is me, but allows me to live from the awareness that I am an extension of God/ Source Energy. What is so beautiful about knowing this is that I now trust the guidance that comes. I call this my Inner Guidance. God knows what I desire most and it is my job to align within and quiet my mind, in order to hear the guidance. Since I am dancing every day, I am able to better hear the inspired actions that my inner guidance is providing for me. When I am willing to take action from this inspired place, my life lines up even better than I could have imagined! Learning to love myself has been about remembering that I am an extension of God/Source Energy, which is Love, and therefore I Am Love as well. This awareness naturally filled the "space" that I spent half of my life trying to fill, but it took all of the experiences in my life so far, to realize this love was inside me all along.

Cassandra Lyons is a Certified Law of Attraction Coach, Author, Interactive Speaker, Dancepreneur, and owner of Be Beautiful You. She inspires people around the World through her project *Dancing 365 Days to Raise Vibration*, by uploading one video per day to YouTube. She invites you to dance with her each day to connect within to your inner guidance, raise your energy, and naturally release resistance. All of Cassandra's programs are created to allow you to connect within, live the life you desire, and shine your beautiful light in the World.
Email: bebeautifulyoucoaching@gmail.com
Website: www.bebeautifulyoucoaching.com

Mari Mitchell

ABOUT MARI MITCHELL

Mari Mitchell is the founder of Dare to be Authentic ™ Radio and the Dare to be Authentic book series. She's a Certified Life Coach and Relationship Coach, founder of Preparing a Path to Love.™ Author, Radio Show Host and Master Angel Card Reader. Her books include *Diary of a Hopeless Romantic*, *Dare to be Authentic Vol. 1 - Finding Your Authentic Self*, and *The Cuban Heart.* Her passion is helping people tap into the majesty that is inside of them to create the life they desire.

Made in the USA
Charleston, SC
16 April 2015